After the Spirit Comes

facts from Acts

by

Roger W. Thomas

You may obtain a 64-page leader's guide and a 32-page activity book to accompany this paperback. Order numbers 1973 and 1587 from Standard Publishing or your local supplier.

New Life
BOOKS™

A Division of Standard Publishing
Cincinnati, Ohio 45231
No. 40049

© 1979, the STANDARD PUBLISHING Company, a division of Standex International Corporation.

Library of Congress Catalog No. 77-83659

ISBN 0-87239-194-9

Printed in U.S.A.   1979

Dedicated to
my co-workers in the faith
Denny Holzbauer and Rusty Martin
and the believers at University Christian
Norman, Oklahoma
a truly Spirit-powered church

"Then was our mouth filled with laughter, and our tongue with singing: then said they among the heathen, The Lord hath done great things for them" (Psalm 126:2, KJV).

Contents

Preface

This is a book about the church! Not the church as it once was, but the church as it is and the church as it can be! The immediate subject of our study will be the *Acts of the Apostles*, a book penned almost two thousand years ago by a physician turned historian named Luke. But our primary interest in studying Luke's account is not to improve our knowledge of ancient history, Roman culture, or even the lives of the early Christian leaders. Our main interest is to discover God's will for His people—the church *today*!

This approach to the book of Acts rests on five basic principles. These principles are the foundation. Everything else depends upon our grasp of these truths.

First, Jesus Christ is alive and well. He was nailed to a cross. He died and was buried. But He arose on the third day just as He had predicted. He then ascended to Heaven and was glorified at the right hand of the heavenly throne! Jesus is alive! He is a fact of history. But He is more than that. He is a factor to be reckoned with today.

Second, because Jesus is alive *today*, He is quite capable of demonstrating His resurrection power in the lives of His people. As living Lord, He bestows gifts on the saints, answers their prayers, and directs their paths according to His perfect will. In short, Jesus keeps His Word: "And surely I will be with you always, to the very end of the age" (Matthew 28:20). "I will not leave you as orphans; I will come to you" (John 14:18).

Third, the Lord's intentional and normal way of demonstrating His resurrection power is through the church. The church, the believing fellowship of the saints, not just the social institution or the ecclesiastical machinery, is God's instrument for changing the world. God never has and never will abandon the church. God's people dare not be less faithful!

Fourth, because the living Lord is very much involved in the lives of His people, the church is by definition a "spiritual community." It was the coming of the Spirit that gave birth to the church, and it is the presence of the Spirit that gives the church purpose and power. Ultimately, it is not the church's wealth, her well-oiled machinery, the brilliance of her scholars, or the political savvy of her leaders that gives the church power, but the reality of the Spirit's presence. The church that will change the world in the first or twentieth century is the Spirit-filled church!

Finally, the God-intended nature and mission of the church today can be discovered only returning to the New Testament. A contractor who is erecting a skyscraper may call for a carpenter or a plumber when he needs their skills. But if he wants to know what the building is supposed to look like or how it's to be put together or what materials are to be used, he goes straght to the architect or to the architect's plans. Likewise, a twentieth-century man who wants to know what the church is and how it was designed to function need not go to the pages of church history, to the great creeds of the faith, or to the sociologist's case book. The church has only one designer and one set of plans. Creeds, church history, and sociology may and do have their places. But they don't define the church as God meant it to be!

Collectively these five principles lead to the theme of this study, *After the Spirit Comes*. In the following chapters we will search the book of Acts for clues about the church's nature and mission today. Above all, we'll look for the work of the Spirit in the life of the church. We'll see how the Spirit (the presence of the resurrected Jesus) worked in the church and how the Spirit-filled church responded to that resurrection power to change the world.

Obviously, we will not be able to consider in detail everything preserved in the book of Acts. We won't even try. Rather, we will simply scale the peaks, consider the high points, and from these points view the vast panorama of the first-century church.

Our purpose is simply to become the church today: to become all that God meant the church to be and to do all that He has called us to do!

I
The Spirit-powered Church
Acts 1

What is it that makes the church go? If we were talking about a machine we'd know the answer. My car has to have gas to go. The refrigerator needs electricity. Even the human body requires food and water in order to function properly. Withhold those vital ingredients and our bodies become powerless, even lifeless.

But the church is not a machine or even a body in the literal and physical sense. So what is it that makes the church go? What is it that gives power and life to the church? The book of Acts answers that question. And it is that answer that we will consider throughout this study.

The church described in Acts is a *Spirit-powered* church. The living presence of Jesus Christ at work in the church is its source of power and life. Remove that source of power or ignore it and the church becomes a lifeless institution. Only as the church is empowered by Jesus' resurrection Spirit can it hope to make a significant difference in the world!

The Acts of the Holy Spirit

The work of the Holy Spirit is so central to Acts that some have suggested that a more appropriate title for Luke's treatise would be "The Acts of the Holy Spirit." The book begins with Jesus instructing the apostles "through the Holy Spirit" (1:2). Before His departure He promised the disciples "power when the Holy Spirit comes" (1:8). Ten days later the events of Pentecost fulfilled that promise (2:1-13). From the beginning to the end, Acts calls attention to the work of the Spirit.

The Spirit's ministry touched every area of Christian activity—evangelism, stewardship, problem solving, leadership selection, and more. Luke was well aware of this. He knew that it was not the brilliance of her leadership, the courage of the apostles, the beautiful architecture of her meeting place, or the wealth of her members that impelled the church across the face of the Roman Empire. The church had something better: an abiding, unshakable conviction that Jesus was alive and working in the world through the Holy Spirit. The believers knew that they were in partnership with God. They were simply to obey in faith and leave the rest to Him.

Acts: the Bridge Book

Acts is a historical book, but it's more than that. Like the Gospels, it is history with a purpose. Many things happened in the first thirty years of the church's life that Luke didn't write about. He was selective. He recorded certain events and ignored others.

In a sense, Luke builds a bridge with Acts. In his Gospel he shows the beginnings of the faith—the birth, life, teachings, death, and resurrection of Jesus. In Acts, Luke explains how the gospel moved from that empty tomb in Jerusalem to a prison house in Rome. He erects a bridge to span the thirty years following the departure of Jesus. Luke's historical bridge provides a vital link between:

Christ and the church. Acts explains how a small band of disciples became a world-wide fellowship of churches. Considered together, Luke and Acts dispel any notion that the church was an afterthought conjured up by Jesus' misguided followers.

Jesus and the Spirit. Luke describes the work of the Spirit as a continuation of Jesus' ministry. The Spirit was promised by Jesus and came only after Jesus was glorified (John 7:39; 16:7). Whenever the Spirit acted in power, the message of Jesus was preached. The bond between Christ and this Spirit is so close that the Spirit is termed "the Spirit of Jesus" (Acts 16:7).

Jew and Gentile. More than anything else, Acts is the bridge between the Jewish disciples and the growing Gentile face of the early church. Luke records the events that brought the first non-Jews into the church, the problems that this created for many Jewish churches, and the eventual decision by the Christian leaders to take the whole gospel to the whole world. The continued opposition to the gospel provides an important sub-theme for Luke's history of the church.

Faith and history. Acts also bridges the gulf between the message of faith and the events of history. The people and places in Luke's record are real. They occupied space and time. The cities they lived in, the rivers they crossed, and the kings who ruled them were all real. Acts is the flesh and bones that give substance to the rest of the New Testament.

The individual and the community. Acts is a church-centered book. It demonstrates the corporative nature of Christianity. Believers in Acts ate together, worshiped together, prayed together, faced death together. They knew they belonged together. Acts unites the faith of the individual Christian and the fellowship of the body.

The ideal and the real. Finally, Acts provides a bridge between the ideal church that we wish existed and the church as it really is. The church Luke describes was far from perfect, but it was used of God and empowered by the Spirit. In our zeal to return the twentieth-century church to her first-century roots, Acts serves as an ever-present reminder that the secret of the church's life, then as now, is not its perfection, but the presence of the living God. Restoring the church always involves a renewal of the Spirit, not just a reorganization of outward forms.

The Ingredients of a Spirit-powered Church

Acts 1 pictures the church behind the church. Like a tiny baby still in its mother's womb, the church before Pentecost was waiting to be born. Yet even then the church bore all the features that so clearly marked its life to come. These pre-Pentecost features are always a part of a Spirit-powered church.

An apostolic church. It was no accident that Luke began his history of the church with the apostles at Jesus' feet. Jesus himself had chosen and taught these men. They were His guarantee that the church would teach what He taught and live what He lived. Throughout Acts, the apostles (the twelve) performed a fivefold ministry: They 1) witnessed to the truth of the resurrection, 2) verified the teachings of Jesus, 3) served as missionaries, heralding the gospel in new places, 4) demonstrated the power of God through signs and miracles, and 5) aided the church in decision making.

Jesus had chosen twelve disciples as a living symbol of the church's identity as the new Israel. For this reason a successor was chosen for Judas. This successor, like the others, had been a follower of Jesus and a personal witness of the resurrection. Together these twelve men formed the foundation upon which the church grew. Jesus was the cornerstone, and they were Jesus' men (Ephesians 2:20). After their passing, there would never again be apostles in the fullest sense of the term. There might be missionaries, and even miracle workers, but never divinely appointed witnesses of the resurrection.

Today's church remains apostolic, not by calling its leaders apostles or performing apostle-like miracles, but by adhering faithfully to the message and witness of THE apostles as recorded in the new covenant Scriptures.

A witnessing church. "You will be my witnesses," was Jesus' parting word to His disciples. The Spirit-powered church described in Acts saw in this commission her reason for existing. The witness they bore was to Jesus, the Messiah and resurrected Lord. Everywhere these early believers went, they carried the same testimony: "Jesus is alive! Jesus is Lord!"

A missionary church. The church's witness was *about* Jesus and *for* the world. Jerusalem was only the beginning. All men were meant to hear the gospel regardless of race, education, social status, or other man-made divisions. This lesson came hard for some in the church, but eventually that fledgling fellowship spanned the empire. A Spirit-powered church is a church with a mission.

A praying church. Prayer was to the early church what breathing is to the body. It was a natural part of life. Each time the fellowship met as recorded in the early chapters of Acts, they met with prayer (Acts 1:14, 24; 2:42; 4:24-30). They truly believed that God heard and answered their requests.

A Scriptural church. When the time came to select a replacement for Judas, Peter called attention to Scripture. This pattern continued throughout Acts. The Scriptures were used to support Christian teaching in all matters of faith and practice. Even the presence of

12

inspired apostles and the existence of spiritual gifts did not remove the need to look to Scripture for divine guidance.

A gathering church. Those early believers knew that to survive they needed each other. So in obedience to Jesus' command they waited, and they waited *together.* Later they would continue to gather for prayer, praise, and teaching. That's how a Spirit-powered church always lives—together in mutual dependence and fellowship.

II
No Longer Orphans
Acts 2

Have you ever been lonely? I mean really lonely. Perhaps you're away from home, traveling by yourself. You sit at the airport waiting for your flight, but all you can think about is your loved ones at home.

Or you may be the one at home. Your husband or wife is gone and you're left in the house alone. You can almost hear the silence.

That's the way the disciples felt. For three years Jesus had been the center of their lives. They had traveled with Him, lived with Him, and listened to His marvelous teachings. But suddenly He was dead. Their lives were shattered.

Then just as suddenly He was alive again! Resurrected from the dead! They could harldy believe it!

Too Good to Be True

During those forty days after Jesus' resurrection the disciples must have kept pinching themselves to be sure they weren't dreaming. But it was true. Jesus was alive! When He talked they listened. Like empty sponges, they soaked up every word He said. They were determined to make up for all those times they had not really paid attention before.

But their joy began to fade when He told them He was leaving. He wasn't always going to be with them as He was at the time. They must have dreaded the day of His leaving. But finally it arrived. He quietly talked with them as He had often done before. When He finished, He began to rise from the ground. Higher and higher He went until a cloud hid Him from view. They just stared, waiting for Him to reappear. But He didn't. He was gone!

What loneliness they must have felt then! The brighter the light, the more intense the darkness seems when it is gone. They were alone, really alone! Disciples without a teacher, children without a father. Orphans!

Don't Forget the Promise

But the loneliness was short-lived. "Do not leave Jerusalem," He had said, "but wait for the gift my Father promised, which you have heard me speak about. For John baptized with water, but in a few days you will be baptized with the Holy Spirit. . . . But you will receive power when the Holy Spirit comes on you; and you will be my witnesses in Jerusalem, and in all Judea and Samaria, and to the ends of the earth" (Acts 1:4, 5, 8).

Earlier he had told them they would be "clothed with power from on high" (Luke 24:49). They remembered His words in the upper room, "I will ask the Father, and he will give you another Counselor, the Spirit of truth, to be with you forever. The world cannot accept this Counselor, because it neither sees him nor knows him. But you know him, for he lives with you and will be in you. I will not leave you as orphans; I will come to you" (John 14:16-18).

15

The God of Great Surprises

The disciples waited for ten days. And then it happened! Regardless of what they had expected, this must have been a surprise. Three miraculous events occurred: 1) a wind-like sound filled the air, 2) cloven tongues like fire rested upon them, and 3) they began "declaring the wonders of God" in languages they had never learned.

Needless to say, the crowd that gathered to investigate the commotion was surprised as well. But even by miracles, some of these Jews were not easily impressed. Many were bewildered by what they saw and heard. Others mocked. A few even suggested that the disciples were drunk.

The Day After Christmas

The real secret of Pentecost, however, was not the wind, fire, or languages. God had poured out his Spirit just as He had promised. That was the most important thing! Peter pointed to Joel's prophecy and said, "This is what was spoken." God had done what He had said He would do!

Unfortunately, many read Luke's record and react to the Pentecostal events like a child on the day after Christmas. The small child becomes so infatuated with the boxes and the wrapping paper that he almost forgets the real gifts. The miracles of Pentecost were mere wrapping paper. The gift was the outpoured Spirit—the presence of the resurrected Lord himself! How tragic for a person to disregard the gift of Pentecost in favor of the wrapping!

Note closely what Peter told the gathered crowd. He didn't exalt the benefits of speaking in other languages. He didn't even testify of the blessings this experience had brought to his life. He told them about Jesus! He explained that all of this had happened for one reason—Jesus, the same Jesus they had crucified, was really the Messiah. God had raised Him from the dead. Now that He was glorified, He had poured out the Holy Spirit just as the prophets had foretold.

How to Receive the Spirit

The query of Peter's hearers was a natural one, "What must we do?" Peter had just told them that Jesus was the Messiah. Not only that, but the resurrected Messiah had ascended to Heaven and poured out the Holy Spirit, just as Joel had promised centuries before.

Peter's answer was short and to the point: "Repent and be baptized, every one of you, in the name of Jesus Christ so that your sins may be forgiven. And you will recieve the gift of the Holy Spirit. The promise is for you and your children and for all who are far off—for all whom the Lord our God will call" (2:38, 39).

One Way—His Way

The blessings of Pentecost are, according to Peter, available only in Jesus. It was no accident that Peter announced baptism "in the name of Jesus Christ." He wanted to make it perfectly clear that no one could share in the life of the Spirit apart from Jesus. The curious may have asked about the strange tongues and the wind-sound, but Peter told them about Jesus. He is the *only* way. His death, resurrection, and glorification are God's answer for guilty men. Forgiveness of sin and the life-giving presence of the Spirit come in the same way—through what Jesus has done! Unless a man comes to Jesus, there can be no redemption, no gift of the Spirit, and no part in the kingdom of God.

About Face—Forward March

Receiving the Spirit requires repentance. In the language of the Bible, repentance is a two-dimensional term. It involves a change of thinking and a change of life. Repentance is a spiritual "about face"—a total change in direction, internally and externally. According to Paul, repentance involves turning to God and proving our repentance with deeds (Acts 26:20). Because the Spirit of God is the Holy Spirit, it is impossible for Him to dwell in a life that has been unholy unless there is a radical change in direction and conduct.

Burning Our Bridges Behind Us

At Pentecost, sharing in the Spirit involved another act—Christian baptism. Why baptism? Partly because baptism is the believer's "show and tell." It is both public and personal. It involves both the will and the body. But more than that, Christian baptism is a radical declaration that the believer's only way to God is through the death, burial, and resurrection of Jesus (Romans 6:1-11). By baptism, we spiritually bury our "old man." We claim God's promise to make us into new creatures after the image of Jesus.

Only in Christianity does baptism have this depth of meaning, but the act itself was nothing new to the Jews. For centuries they had practiced various ritual cleansings, including immersion. Many scholars think that even before the time of Christ total immersion in water had become a part of the ceremony by which a non-Jewish convert became an official part of the Jewish community. Certainly such immersion was practiced a few centuries later. The Gentile's baptism was an acknowledgement of his own impurity as well as an inauguration into the family of God.

John the Baptist boldly told the sons of Abraham that baptism was just as necessary for them as it was for a pagan sinner (Matthew 3:7-12). At Pentecost Peter said the same thing. The Jews needed forgiveness, and it could be received only through the very

Galilean whom they had crucified a few weeks earlier. For those Jewish listeners, baptism was a dramatic declaration that they couldn't save themselves by their religious traditions, their family heritage, or their good deeds. By baptism in Jesus' name they burned their bridges behind them. They confessed that the only way to God and the only way to share in the blessings of the Spirit was through the sacrifice of Jesus.

After the Spirit Comes (Acts 2:42-47)

Pentecost, A. D. 30, marked the beginning of God's fulfillment of His promise to pour out His Spirit on all flesh. What happened in the life of that early church after Pentecost provides a clear indication of what God always wants to happen after the Spirit comes.

First, the individual believers were drawn into a close supportive fellowship. They met together, they ate together, and they shared together. The Spirit left little room for the idea that a "spiritual" man is self-sufficient. Quite to the contrary, the truly "Spirit-filled" man recognized that he needed the fellowship and strength of other Christians.

Second, the members of this spiritual fellowship described in Acts 2 demonstrated their love for one another in practical ways. Those who had more than they needed shared with those who lacked. The result—everyone's needs were met. Unselfish concern for others is one evidence of the Spirit's presence. Human religion often leads men to withdraw into a shell of personal piety. The Spirit frees men from that shell, frees them to think of others and then to move to meet the needs of others.

Third, the church was a worshiping community. Prayer and praise to God marked their assemblies and their individual lives. Jesus said that the Comforter would seek to glorify the Son and the Son the Father. Likewise, individuals indwelled by the Spirit are always pointing upward, not inward. They want men to see God, not themselves. Their testimony is not "Look how good I am," but rather "Look, God is good!"

Fourth, the Spirit led the church to the Word, in this case the apostles' teachings. The Holy Spirit does the same thing today. He directs men to the Scriptures, not away from them. No measure of spirituality, not even "charismatic" gifts, can be a substitute for a deep personal knowledge of Scripture.

Finally, after the Spirit came the church became involved in the "soul-saving" business. They wanted everyone to know what they knew and to experience the joyous life with God that they now shared. Evangelism, the winning of lost men and women to faith in Jesus Christ, is a work of the Spirit.

III

The Gospel According to the Holy Spirit

Act 3

What Do You Say to a Lost Man?

Like the church of Acts, we live in a lost world. Sin, guilt, and rebellion against God abound. Millions die "without hope and without God" (Ephesians 2:12). What does the church say to such a world? What is our message to those who surround us? What is it that the church must preach if it never does anything else? Acts answers these questions.

The Holy Spirit's Sermon Book

Acts is a history book, but also a sermon book. Almost half its chapters contain sermons preached by early Christian spokesmen—Peter, Paul, Stephen, and others. Note briefly the major sermons recorded in Acts.

2:14-39. To the Jerusalem crowd, Peter explains the outpouring of the Holy Spirit. He says the miracles of that day were foretold by the prophets and made possible by Jesus, the resurrected and glorified Messiah. Jesus is the one the Old Testament predicted and the one whose claims were vindicated by the resurrection. Therefore it is plain that God has made Him "both Lord and Christ."

3:12-26. The healing of a lame man provides Peter an opportunity to talk about Jesus. Faith in the name of the glorified, resurrected Jesus healed the man. Jesus has been crucified, but the God of the fathers has raised him up. Forgiveness is available to any who will repent and turn to God. Those who will not listen to Jesus will be cut off.

4:8-12. In his Spirit-filled defense before the Sanhedrin, Peter claims again that the name of Jesus healed the lame man. Jesus is the stone rejected by men but selected by God. Salvation is found in none other.

5:29-32. Again Peter announces that God raised Jesus from the dead. He is exalted as Prince and Savior and now offers repentance and forgiveness to Israel.

7:2-53. Stephen traces the acts of God in history from Abraham to Jesus. He insists that the Jews have always resisted the Holy Spirit and have done so again by crucifying Jesus and rejecting the message of His resurrection.

10:34-43. Peter explains to Cornelius the beginning of the gospel. He tells of Jesus' ministry, His death and resurrection, and His commission to preach the gospel to the people. He says the prophets foretold that forgiveness of sins would come to anyone who would believe on the Messiah.

13:16-41. In the synagogue at Pisidian Antioch, Paul recounts the blessings that God has bestowed on Israel. Out of this heritage was born Jesus, the prophesied Messiah. The people of Jerusalem rejected Him and asked Pilate to execute Him. He died, but God raised Him from the tomb. Now through this Jesus forgiveness is offered to all.

14:15-17. As a pagan crowd in Lystra prepares to offer sacrifices to them as gods, Paul and Barnabas contend that they are not gods, but messengers of the living God. This God wants the worship of these pagans. Once He let them do as they pleased, but even then He blessed them through His creation.

17:22-31. To the Athenian intellectuals, Paul proclaims the God they know nothing about. He is the sovereign Creator of the universe. He now calls all men to repentance in preparation for the day of judgment. The resurrected Jesus will be the judge on that last day.

20:18-35. Paul tells the Christian leaders of Ephesus of his willingness to face hardships in order to share the gospel. He reminds them of his work with the churches and commends them to the Holy Spirit in their future labors.

22:3-21. Paul shares his personal testimony with a mob in the temple court. He tells of his conversion from a persecutor to a preacher of Jesus' gospel.

26:2-23. Paul's legal defense before King Agrippa includes the account of his conversion and subsequent labors as a preacher of the gospel. He insists that all he has preached is completely consistent with the message of Moses and the prophets—the Messiah would suffer, be raised from the dead, and then be preached to Jew and Gentile alike.

28:17-28. Representatives of the Roman Jewish community gather to hear the visitor from Jerusalem. Paul contends that Jesus fulfilled the predictions of Moses and the prophets. He warns that Jewish rejection of Jesus will simply speed the gospel on to the Gentiles.

A Simple Gospel

A young minister in a college town was embarrassed by the thought of criticism from his highly educated congregation. He sought counsel from his father, an old and wise minister.

"Father, I am hampered in my preaching. If I cite anything from geology, there is Professor A, a teacher of that science, right before me. If I use an illustration from Roman mythology there is Professor B, ready to trip me for any little mistake. If I cite something from literature that pleases me, I am confronted by a learned man that teaches that subject. What shall I do?"

The wise old man replied, "Don't be discouraged. Just preach the gosepl; they probably know little of that."

The gospel according to the Holy Spirit contains one basic theme—Jesus. The apostles who heralded that message may have known many other subjects, but before a lost world they had only one message. Religion, theology, personal experiences, and even miracles may have had their places; but they were not the gospel, nor a substitute for it.

The Gospel Is a Person

The Christian message is Jesus. Paul could say, "Jews demand miraculous signs and Greeks look for wisdom, but we preach Christ crucified" (1 Corinthians 1:22, 23). Christianity is a relationship with the resurrected Christ.

The preaching of Acts virtually overflows with references to the person of Jesus, as we have seen from our survey of the sermons. Look again at the details about Jesus in one of those messages. In his sermon at Solomon's Colonnade (Acts 3:12-26), Peter used several terms for Jesus that help to summarize the gospel.

Christ (3:18). Peter called Jesus the Christ, the anointed Messiah of God. He is the one whom God's people had looked forward to for generations. Jesus,

24

and no one else, fulfilled all of the Old Testament prophecies.

Prophet Like Moses (3:22; Deuteronomy 18:15, 18, 19). Jesus was the fulfillment of the law that had been given through Moses. He was the heavenly spokesman. When He taught, men were to listen. Men's response to Jesus' teachings and claims would determine their eternal destiny.

Author of Life (3:15). Jesus is the source of all life. "Through him all things were made; without him nothing was made that has been made. In him was life, and that life was the light of men" (John 1:3, 4). Jesus is also the beginning of the resurrection life. Men killed Him; but He arose again, vindicating His claim to give life to others.

Servant (3:13, 26). Jesus was totally faithful to His divine mission. Though He is divine in every way, He demonstrated the mind of a servant. In so doing, He gave flesh to Isaiah's prediction of a suffering servant who could save the people (Isaiah 53:4-9).

Holy and Righteous One (3:14). Jesus perfectly demonstrated the life that pleases God. He harmed no one and committed no crimes. Yet He died a sinner's death. His sinlessness justifies His position as the final judge of all men.

In these titles, Peter brought together the great claims about Jesus: 1) He fulfilled the Messianic prophecies of the Old Testament, 2) He died on the cross for our sins, 3) He arose again and was glorified in Heaven, and 4) He will one day appear again as judge of all. This is the gospel—the person of Jesus, who He is, what He did, and what He is going to do!

The Gospel Is a Fact

The preaching of the apostles insisted that Jesus was a real person of history, not just a myth or creation of overzealous followers. The disciples were witnesses of His life, and so were countless others who were not believers (Acts 2:22). The Christians claimed that what they preached was historically verifiable. Eyewitnesses abounded. The belief or unbelief of their listeners did not change the reliability of the message. The gospel—the facts about Jesus—was to be accepted, not because it sounded nice or promised happy lives to people, but because it was *true*!

The Gospel Is a Gift

The gospel is not what man must do to appease God, but what God has done in Christ to reconcile man to himself. This is the good news—forgiveness of sins offered to all men. Jesus' death, not man's righteousness or labors for God, is what saves.

The Gospel Is a Relationship

Christianity is a relationship with Jesus. "Christ in you, the hope of glory" (Colossians 1:27) is the good news. Faith brings one into this saving relationship. Since it is a relationship, it is a growing, learning experience, not an act that one does once and then forgets. The cross is the key to the relationship.

Preaching the Gospel Today

The gospel is Jesus, not religious ritual, theological opinion, or personal experience! What does this truth say to the life of the church today?

First, we must recognize the difference between preaching and teaching. Sometimes the two are done together, and often our common speech makes no distinction between them. But here *preaching* means evangelizing, telling the good news. Preaching is heralding Jesus—His claims and His promises. Talk is not preaching just because it is done from a pulpit. The word *preaching*, proclaiming the gospel, refers to the message, not the method.

Second, this distinction is important because it is the gospel that must be shared with the unsaved. Men are not saved by accepting teachings, but by believing the gospel. It is very easy for a Christian to think that he must know everything in the Bible before he can speak to the lost. Not so! One need only know the gospel. That's what convicts, converts, and saves, not our intellectual arguments or theological speculations.

Does this mean that Christians need not care about knowing the Bible thoroughly or becoming acquainted with the intellectual questions that non-Christians raise? Not at all! This emphasis on the *gospel* simply means that all else is secondary as far as saving the lost is concerned. Anything else we say must lead to a clear presentation of the deeds and claims of Jesus. We have not shared the gospel until we have talked about Jesus.

Third, the gospel is the basis of Christian fellowship. A man is my brother in the Lord because we agree on Jesus, not because we agree on every jot and tittle of theology. A man may be wrong (from my perspective) about almost everything else; but if he is right about Jesus, that man is still my brother. But if a man is wrong about Jesus and right about everything else in the Bible, he is still not my spiritual brother. We are brothers when we embrace the same Savior.

IV
The Spark of Heaven
Acts 2, 3

In the city square in my home town is a huge old cannon, the kind used in the Civil War. Once that cannon was the most potent weapon in a military arsenal. With its great barrel pointing toward the sky, it could send a steel ball hurtling behind enemy lines.

But even when new, the barrel of that great cannon was powerless by itself. Birds could nest in it without fear. Without the cannon balls and the charge of powder the gun was useless. But even powder and ball were not enough. The artillery gunner could carefully load the charge and place the ball in the proper position and still do no damage to the foe. Only when the spark of fire was applied to the powder did that great cannon with its death-dealing shells became an instrument of power.

"If It Is From God"

The church and that ancient cannon have much in common. By itself, the church in Acts posed little threat to anyone. Its leaders were a handful of unlearned Galileans, none of whom were particularly known for bravery. The church had little money and hardly any influence among the religious leaders of the day. No one could have guessed that within a generation that insignificant little "Jewish sect" would spread its teaching across the seas and into the power center of the empire.

Gamaliel was right! The Jewish leader may not have fully understood his own words when he advised the Sanhedrin to free the apostles, but his words were prophetic. "Leave these men alone! Let them go!" he advised. "For if their purpose or activity is of human origin, it will fail. But if it is from God, you will not be able to stop these men; you will only find yourselves fighting against God" (Acts 5:38, 39).

The secret of the church in Acts was not its leaders, its wealth, its influence, or its organization. It was God! The spark of Heaven, God's supernatural presence, ignited the life of the church and made it a powerful part of God's cosmic arsenal.

A Miracle a Day

Acts is a miraculous book. Page after page is filled with mighty wonders and signs. The sick were healed (9:32-35, 19:11, 12; 28:7-10), the lame were made to walk (3:1-10), demons were cast out (8:4-8; 16:16-18), and the dead were restored to life (9:36-40).

The Testimony of God

Why the miracles in Acts? Luke merely records the events. He offers little information about how the miracles were performed, the reasons behind them, or the long-term results. One explanation for the miracles is found in Acts 14:3: "Paul and Barnabas spent considerable time there, speaking boldly for the Lord, who confirmed the message of his grace by enabling them to do miraculous signs and wonders.'

29

Hebrews 2:3, 4 declares the same truth, "This salvation, which was first announced by the Lord, was confirmed to us by those who heard him. God also testified to it by signs, wonders, and various miracles, and gifts of the Holy Spirit distributed according to his will." The miracles performed by the apostles and others were God's testimony added to that of His spokesmen.

Our Problem With Miracles

Modern people, including many Christians, have a real problem believing in miracles. We acknowledge that such events happened two thousand years ago. But today? That's another matter. Our problem comes not so much from the Bible as from the humanistic bent of our society. Nowhere does the Bible suggest that God has stopped answering the prayers of His saints or working in their lives.

Many of us have almost become deists in our view of God. The classic deist insisted that God created the world, wound it up like a cosmic clock, and then set it on the mantle to operate by itself. To the deist, any intervention from God was totally unthinkable. The deist's modern counterpart in the church often adds a subtle twist to the scheme. Rather than a watchmaker, the Creator is imagined as a publisher. God created the universe, worked in the lives of the patriarchs and prophets, visited earth as the Son, inspired the Scriptures, and then left. We are now on our own without any hope that God is actually involved in this world. Nonsense!

How to Tell the Wolves From the Sheep

A part of our reluctance to openly accept God's power today comes from our knowledge that many who are obviously false teachers claim miraculous ability. Rather than "test the spirits" as the Bible admonishes (1 John 4:1), we simply reject (or define away) the Spirit.

The ability to perform miracles (or appear to perform them) is not proof that one is sanctioned by God. Remember Jesus' words? "Watch out for false prophets. They come to you in sheep's clothing, but inwardly they are ferocious wolves. By their fruit you will recognize them. . . . Not everyone who says to me, 'Lord, Lord' will enter the kingdom of heaven, but only he who does the will of my Father who is in heaven. Many will say to me on that day, 'Lord, Lord, did we not prophesy in your name, and in your name drive out demons and perform many miracles?' Then I will tell them plainly, 'I never knew you. Away from me, you evildoers!' " (Matthew 7:15-23).

In Acts, at least three persons other than the apostles and Christian messengers are credited with miraculous power or the appearance of it. Simon, the Samaritan sorcerer, had a large following because of his amazing magical abilities (8:9-11). Whether his power was mere trickery or of Satan, Luke does not say. The effect was the same in either case. Bar-Jesus, the attendant to Sergius Paulus, proconsul of Paphos, apparently had similar powers. In this case, Paul labeled Bar-Jesus "a child of the devil" (13:10). In Philippi, Paul and Silas encountered a slave girl with the supernatural ability to foretell the future. Her powers were clearly demonic (16:16-18).

Tests of the Spirits

Scripture suggests three primary tests of the spirits:

1. Does the "miracle worker" confess Jesus as Lord? According to Paul, "No one who is speaking by the Spirit of God says, 'Jesus be cursed,' and no one can say, 'Jesus is Lord' except by the Holy Spirit" (1 Corinthians 12:3). John adds, "This is how you can recognize the Spirit of God: Every spirit that acknowl-

edges that Jesus Christ has come in the flesh is from God, but every spirit that does not acknowledge Jesus is not from God. This is the spirit of the antichrist, which you have heard is coming and even now is already in the world" (1 John 4:2, 3).

2. Does the "miracle worker" seek to live a God-honoring life? As Jesus phrased it, "By their fruit you will recognize them" (Matthew 7:20).

3. Does the "miracle worker" acknowledge and teach the apostles' doctrine? John said, "We are from God, and whoever knows God listens to us; but whoever is not from God does not listen to us. This is how we recognize the Spirit of truth and the spirit of falsehood" (1 John 4:6). To the Corinthians Paul wrote, "If anybody thinks he is a prophet or spiritually gifted, let him acknowledge that what I am writing to you is the Lord's command" (1 Corinthians 14:37).

The Test of Money

A Christian document from the early second century known as the *Didache* or "The Teachings of the Lord to the Gentiles by the Twelve Apostles" suggests another test for a prophet. According to the *Didache*, if an apostle or prophet comes in the name of the Lord, he should be received. However, if the would-be prophet or apostle stays for more than two days he is a false prophet. If he tells you to give silver or gold to the needy his advice should be heeded. If, however, he instructs you to give it to him, he is a false prophet. The Didache is of unknown origin and certainly uninspired, but its test of money is worthy of consideration.

Power Unlimited (Do We All Have to Walk on Water?)

We are convinced that God is still on the throne of Heaven and working in the lives of His people. Does this mean that we should expect to see the same miracles today that occurred in the first-century church? If the twentieth-century church is to restore the life of the first-century church, must apostolic-style miracles be repeated? These are important questions that reflect on our entire approach to the book of Acts and more specifically our understanding of the Spirit's work.

Any Bible answer to these questions must first affirm that God is free! He is not limited to our wishes, our understanding, or our expectations! If He wishes to work a miracle He can. If He doesn't wish to, He doesn't have to. The Lord is the real miracle worker—not men, not even the apostles. Luke insisted on this when he wrote that *the Lord* confirmed the apostles' message by enabling them to do signs and wonders (Acts 14:3). He was the one at work! Peter affirmed this when he explained the healing of the lame man to the temple crowd (Acts 3:12, 13, 16).

Second, the Bible rejects the idea that God is a creature of habit, that He always works the same way. Jesus is the same yesterday, today, and forever (Hebrews 13:8); but that doesn't mean that what God did through Moses He must do today.

This should be obvious to any student of Bible history. The Scriptures cover thousands of years of human history. Yet most of the miracles recorded in the Bible are clustered in three very narrow time periods: the time of Moses and Joshua, the ministries of Elijah and Elisha, and the events of the Gospels and Acts. Not much is said about miracles occurring during the many other centuries of Bible history.

Does this mean that miracles never occurred at any other time or that they can't occur today? Not at all! This fact merely teaches us that miracles are God's *exceptional* work. He can always do them, but most of the time He doesn't—at least as far as the Bible's record is concerned. The miracles that are recorded in the Bible were generally "signs," special wonders designed to call attention to a new chapter in God's unfolding drama of redemption. Moses was the lawgiver, Elijah and Elisha were the greatest of the prophets, and Jesus was the fulfillment of both the law and the prophets.

God works through diversity (1 Corinthians 12:4-26). The Lord has so constituted the church that we are like a body with many different parts, not an assembly line with identical pieces following one right after the other. The Bible indicates that God's love for diversity affects history as well as His gifts to the church. He has not granted to every age the same demonstration of His power. He is always at work, but not always in the same way!

An absence of "wonders and signs" does not necessarily mean an absence of the Spirit. However, a rejection of the ability of the Spirit to work as He wishes may well be evidence of that very problem!

What Do You Say to a Miracle?

God does perform wonders today. I have every reason to believe He does and no reason to believe He doesn't. However, the power and decision are His, not mine. My task is merely to walk by faith, doing what He has told me to do. Faith means accepting His decision about how He manifests His presence in my life— accepting it without becoming proud if He chooses to perform a miracle or discouraged if He chooses to work through ordinary means. It's His presence that matters most, not His method.

V

Keeping the Church on Fire
Acts 4

Many years ago, five young ministerial students, soon to be ordained, spent a Sunday in London. Anxious to hear some well-known preachers, they made their way to Charles Haddon Spurgeon's famous tabernacle. While they were waiting for the doors to open, a stranger approached and asked, "Gentlemen, would you like to see the heating apparatus of the church?"

They were not particularly anxious to visit a boiler room on a hot July day, but they consented. The stranger, Spurgeon himself, took them down some steps and opened a door. "There, sirs, is our heating apparatus," whispered the great preacher. They saw before them seven hundred believers bowed in prayer seeking the Lord's blessing on the service about to begin in the tabernacle.

If the apostle Peter were giving a guided tour of the early Christian congregations, he might point to a similar scene. Prayer was a vital part of the early church's life. Between the ascension and Pentecost, "They all joined together constantly in prayer" (Acts

1:14). The church prayed when facing decisions, selecting leaders, and commissioning missionaries. In adversity they turned to God for strength and courage. In times of opportunity, they praised Him for His goodness and power. The church of Acts knew that a prayerless church is a powerless church!

John Bunyan, author of *Pilgrim's Progress*, said, "Pray often, for prayer is a shield for the soul, a sacrifice to God, and a scourge for Satan. Prayer is as the pitcher that fetcheth water from the brook, therewith to water the herbs. Break the pitcher and it will fetch no water, and for want of water the garden withers."

The Prayers of the Saints

The first recorded prayer in Acts occurred at the selection of Matthias as Judas' apostolic replacement (Acts 1:24, 25). This was no small matter for the church. They knew that the Lord had made the original decision about the apostles and that He would guide their decision now.

"Lord," they prayed, "you know everyone's heart. Show us which of these two you have chosen to take over this apostolic ministry, which Judas left to go where he belongs." They then drew lots, and the decision was made.

One fact stands out in this example. They were absolutely conviced that the Lord was capable of making a decision and revealing that decision to His people. They did not labor under the illusion that the Lord had abandoned His saints. He was there and He was active. This conviction drew them together in prayer.

Prayer: a Godly Christian Weapon

The next prayer of the saints preserved by Luke was prompted by persecution (Acts 4:23-30). The Jewish leaders warned Peter and John of the consequences that would follow if they persisted in preaching the gospel in Jerusalem. What were they to do? Flee the city? No! Their mission there was not yet complete. Obey the order of the authorities, and disobey the Lord? Impossible! They must stand firm and proclaim the resurrection until every man, woman, and child in the city had heard! But they were humans—weak, doubting, scared humans. They needed help, supernatural help.

"Sovereign Lord," they prayed, "you made the heaven and the earth and the sea, and everything in them. You spoke by the Holy Spirit through the mouth of your servant, our father David: 'Why do the nations rage, and the people plot in vain? The kings of the earth take their stand, and the rulers gather together against the Lord and against his Anointed One.' Indeed Herod and Pointius Pilate met together with the Gentiles and the people of Israel in this city to conspire against your holy servant Jesus, whom you anointed. They did what your power and will had decided beforehand should happen. Now, Lord, consider their threats and enable your servants to speak your word with great boldness. Stretch out your hand to heal and perform miraculous signs and wonders through the name of your holy servant Jesus." God heard the prayer and answered it. With the Spirit guiding, they did speak boldly.

Luther said, "Prayer is a strong wall and fortress for the church; it is a godly Christian weapon." The enemies of the faith may have had swords and spears, but the church had prayer! They knew that the Lord of the universe was behind them. No, they knew *they* were behind Him! The battle belonged to the Lord. They were merely to rely on Him. "Not by might, nor by power, but by my Spirit, says the Lord of hosts" (Zechariah 4:6). This could have been their call to arms.

Prayer and Enemies

Note what they prayed for. They asked God for boldness to speak His word, not for safety. They wanted to be used of Him in the midst of the battle. Neither did they pray that God would destroy their foes. They wanted to convert them, not condemn them.

Madame Chiang Kai-shek, wife of the great Chinese leader, told how her devout Christian mother spent hours in prayer during the Japanese invasion of Manchuria. One day Madame Chiang said to her, "Mother, you are so powerful in prayer, why don't you pray that God will annihilate Japan by an earthquake?"

Her mother looked gravely at her and said, "When you pray or expect me to pray, don't insult God by asking Him to do something that would be unworthy of you, a mortal."

"After that," said Madame Chiang, "I prayed *for* the Japanese people."

First Things First

Luke doesn't preserve an example of the apostles' private prayer lives, but he does record an important fact. When explaining the need for helpers in the ministry of the Jerusalem church, the apostles said, "We will turn this responsibility over to them and *will give our attention to prayer* and the ministry of the word" (Acts 6:3, 4).

An old Judean teacher met a young convert and asked him if he said his prayers regularly.

He answered, "I am a Christian, but I have no time for prayer."

"Then you have no time to breathe," said the teacher.

"Oh, I have to make time for that in order to live."

"My son," said the teacher, "it is just as important to pray as to breathe."

Luther was once asked how he found time to pray so much when he was busy. He replied that it was when he was the busiest that he most needed to pray. "When I have much to do," he said, "I don't have time *not* to pray!"

Prayer—Jesus Style

Stephen demonstrated the mind of Christ in prayer. Even as this first Christian martyr died he turned to the Lord. "Lord Jesus," he prayed, "receive my spirit." Then he fell on his knees and cried out, "Lord, do not hold this sin against them" (Acts 7:57-60).

No wonder the young man standing nearby could never forget that day. Paul was the one who held the garments for those who executed Stephen, and no doubt he later recited this prayer from memory so that Luke could preserve it for history.

Fasting: Prayer's Power Partner

In the early church, prayer was often associated with another spiritual practice now neglected— fasting. The leaders of the Antioch congregation fasted as they commissioned Paul and Barnabas for their first missionary tour. "So after they had fasted and prayed, they placed their hands on them and sent them off" (Acts 13:3). The two missionaries followed the same procedure when they selected local leaders for the churches they established. "Paul and Barnabas appointed elders for them in each church and, with prayer and fasting, committed them to the Lord in whom they had put their trust" (Acts 14:23).

The Scripture abounds with examples of the natural link between prayer and fasting. Apparently the intentional abstinence from food for "spiritual purposes" has great impact on our ability to concentrate on the things of God. Recovering this "lost" art would do much to restore spiritual power to the church.

The Church That Prays Together

Building powerful prayer lives ought to be a goal of every Bible-believing church. Obviously a prayerless church cannot be a Spirit-powered church. Here are some simple suggestions that can strengthen the prayer practices of the average church.

1. Involve the believers in public prayer. It is proper to pray in public. The church in Acts did it (Acts 4:23-30). But if the preacher is the only one who leads the public prayers of the congregation, many will conclude that praying is his business and not theirs. How tragic! Valuable lessons on prayer can be taught by the public example of Christian leaders.

2. Solicit prayer needs and concerns from the congregation. Such a practice makes prayer a part of the "worship service." Our church provides prayer request cards for the worshipers to hand in during the assembly. These then are shared with the entire congregation prior to the prayer time. Such lists can also be published for the benefit of shut-ins and others.

3. Encourage times of special prayer and fasting for the church, such as before the selection of leaders, before revival meetings, prior to special congregational decisions, and when special prayers for healing are in order.

4. Encourage personal and daily prayer in the church. The public prayer practices of the church ought to be but the tip of the iceberg. The constant flow of the prayers of the saints day by day throughout the week is the secret power source of the church.

5. Establish groups of special prayer partners who will pray specifically for others in the church—the preacher while he is calling, college students away from home, or missionaries supported by the church. The list is unlimited!

6. Keep a prayer journal—both privately and congregationally. Many Christians fail to recognize an-

swered prayers because they quickly forget what they prayed for. Keeping a written record of prayer requests and their dates provides a ready source for future praise and thanksgiving.

VI
Living Together in a World Falling Apart
Acts 5, 6

A few years ago American Baptist theologian Harvey Cox spent a summer teaching at the Naropa Buddhist Center. When reporters quizzed him about his experience, he talked not about Buddhist theology, but the sense of community shared by the students of the eastern religion (reported in the *Denver Post* July 8, 1976).

The Harvard professor related his own experience at Naropa to society at large: "People seem to be on a kind of search for what the Buddhists call 'W 'Sango', a search for community, for a fellowship, for a loving and supportive company of brothers and sisters who take you seriously."

Cox then added, "This sort of community seems to be absent from many Christian churches, which are not much more than spiritual filling stations, offering minimum contact." He suggested that Christianity could have a renewed strength and appeal if it would offer the sense of community described in the book of Acts.

One Heart and One Mind

What enabled the church in Acts to become the kind of community that the world is looking for? First, they were one in faith. Consider the oneness of faith and life displayed in the church:

"These all with one mind were continually devoting themselves to prayer" (Acts 1:14, NASV).

"They lifted their voice to God with one accord" (Acts 4:24, NASV).

"And the congregation of those who believed were of one heart and soul" (Acts 4:32, NASV).

The Key to Unity

In geometry, two lines are parallel to one another if they are both parallel to a third line. That's also the formula for Christian unity. The church is knit together by a common commitment to Christ and to the proclamation of the gospel. Unity develops when we realize that we are all in the same family if we all have the same Father. All else becomes secondary to this mutual commitment to Jesus.

The Charismatic Church

The early church's fellowship also resulted from its charismatic nature. The term *charismatic* describes God's grace gifts to His people. According to the Scriptures, God has given differing gifts to the church. Some believers are able to contribute one needed ingredient, while others have different abilities.

We are different because God made us that way. Our differences require that we lean on one another to be all that God intends us to be. Apart we are imperfect, incomplete, isolated parts of a body. Together in Him, we are "joined and held together by every supporting ligament." So the church "grows and builds itself up in love, as each part does its work" (Ephesians 4:16).

Because the believers in Acts were a charismatic (gift-bearing) church they could demonstrate true fellowship and service in the midst of a fragmented world. Each had what the others needed. Unity was a matter of spiritual life or death.

Believe it or not, that is still true today!

Evidences of Fellowship

The fellowship experienced by the first-century church manifested itself in several ways. First, they gathered together frequently, in some cases daily. The purpose of their gatherings varied. Sometimes it was for prayer or worship. Other times they gathered to listen to the apostles' teachings. Occasionally, large numbers of Christians assembled to consider an important decision or hear a report from a traveling evangelist. Often they simply met to share a meal. They met in public halls, the temple, or in each other's homes.

The importance of such gatherings is best illustrated by the words of admonition in Hebrews 10:24, 25: "Let us consider how we may spur one another on toward love and good deeds. Let us not give up meeting together, as some are in the habit of doing, but let us encourage one another—and all the more as you see the Day approaching."

New Testament fellowship was also practical. These Christians were doers, not just hearers of the Word (James 1:22). They met and talked. They ate meals together. But they didn't stop there. When someone had a need, they prayed and they acted. Those who needed financial assistance were taken care of (Acts 4:32—5:11). When the needs of the Greek widows were being neglected, the apostles took the problem seriously (Acts 6:1-7). Later when famine struck Palestine, fellow Christians to the north gathered funds to help their Hebrew brothers through the emergency

(Acts 11:27-30). This practical concern was true fellowship at its best.

Yours, Mine, and His

The Jerusalem Christians met each other's needs by pooling their resources. In so doing, they demonstrated a radically different attitude toward possessions than that normally found in the world, then or now. Most men live out one of four attitudes toward material possessions.

Some men say, "What's mine is mine and what's yours is mine." This is the thief. He recognizes no one else's rights, only his own. What he wants, he takes.

Others say, "What's mine is mine, and what's yours is ours." State socialism! In the name of helping the poor, a bureaucracy takes control of everyone's property and returns it according to the priorities of the state.

Many insist, "What's mine is mine; what's yours is yours. Keep away from mine. I earned it." This is capitalism at its worst: every man for himself. If a man can make a million, so much the better. If he can't even make enough to live on, that's his problem.

A few add, "What's mine is mine. What's yours is yours! If you promise to keep quiet, I'll give you a little, but only after I have all I want." This is the modern welfare system. Of course the other side of the system often says, "What's mine is mine; what's yours is yours. Since you have more than I, you ought to give me some. Just don't expect me to work for it." Both approaches leave a great deal to be desired.

The Christians described in Acts lived by a totally different system. Their attitude is just as foreign to the communist as to the capitalist. They said, "What's mine is God's. If you have a need, I'll share, because that's what *He* wants!" They believed what Jesus had taught: "It is more blessed to give than to receive

45

(Acts 20:35). They knew that the Lord could provide for their every need, so they could afford to be generous.

Only this last attitude can explain the totally selfless actions of Barnabas (Acts 4:36, 37). It also accounts for the seriousness of Ananias' and Sapphira's sin. They sinned against the Holy Spirit, not just against their fellow Christians. They took what was theirs as God's stewards and lied about its use.

The Witness of Love

There is little wonder that these early Christians caught the attention of their society. They were different! Justin Martyr, a second-century Christian leader, explained this difference. "We used to value above all things money and possessions. Now we bring togther all that we have and share it with those who are in need. Formerly we hated and killed one another; and because of a difference in nationality or custom, we refused to admit strangers within our gates. Now since the coming of Christ, we all live in peace. We pray for our enemies and seek to convert those who hate us unjustly." Tertullian, another second-century believer, wrote, "It is our care for the helpless, our practice of loving kindness, that brands us in the eyes of many of our opponents. 'Only look,' they say, 'Look how they love one another.' " (*Apology* XXXIX).

Developing a Fellowshipping Church

What can a modern church do to rekindle this sense of fellowship experienced by the New Testament church? Here are some suggestions:

Develop a charismatic consciousness in the church. Teach and preach that God does give ministry abilities to His people. (See Romans 12:3-8.) Encourage every Christian to find an avenue of service to others. Recognize those who provide such ministries as giving, mercy, and hospitality rather than just preaching and teaching.

Become burden-bearers. Encourage those with needs to share their problems with the church. Assume responsibility for the financial needs of those in the fellowship. A portion of the church budget might be set aside for helping members (and non-members) with financial emergencies. Clothing rooms and food pantries can be established to help with those needs. Most of all, these things must be done without apology. They are a valid part of the Biblical church's ministry.

Play together. The church must get together to do "people things," not just study, worship, and plan. Recreation and athletics can be a valid part of church life if they are used to develop fellowship.

Eat together. The early Christians broke bread together. They knew that something special happens when people share a meal. Regular all-church meals are valid if we understand why we have them. An even better idea is to encourage Christians to invite new members and neighbors into their homes for meals. Some congregations divide their membership into small groups that are asked to meet together at least once a month for a meal.

Get out of the church house. Nothing can inhibit true fellowship like a church building. Revolutionary things have happened in churches that have abandoned a building-centered program in favor of a series of "house church" meetings. The traditional midweek prayer meeting in many churches can easily be transformed into home prayer gatherings.

Live together. Christian communities in which several single Christians or even families share a house have sprung up all over the country. While this may still be a bit radical for many, it is worthy of consideration in our "fellowship-less" society. Dave and Neta

Jackson's book *Living Together in a World Falling Apart* (Creation House, 1974) discusses the exciting possibilities of such "extended" Christian households.

Weekend retreats and all-day church gatherings provide a less extreme opportunity for Christians to live together. Such occasions allow believers to see each other as they really are and to better understand each other's needs as fellow humans.

Think together. An important part of fellowship is the freedom to think and question openly. Steps can be taken to allow all the members to feel that they have a voice in the life of the church. All-church planning sessions can be scheduled. Some churches periodically have special Sunday-evening programs devoted completely to "question and answer" sessions with the preacher and elders. Bible questions, doctrinal issues, church programs, and personal problems are discussed in an open and gracious manner. Fellowship thrives in the atmosphere created by such gatherings.

VII
The Acts of God
Acts 7

The church in Acts was a Bible church. The early disciples accepted the authority of Scripture. They preached its message to others and turned to it for guidance. The Scriptures were important because in them was preserved the record of God's dealing with man.

The Bible of the early church was what we call the Old Testament, though they never would have thought of calling it that. Eventually the writings of Paul, Peter, and others in the apostolic company became a part of the Christian Scriptures. These were not yet written when the church began, but this presented little problem. Eyewitnesses of the faith abounded. The acts and teachings of Jesus were still a part of public knowledge.

Beyond that, the early Christians knew that the Old Testament Scriptures contained the roots of the gospel. They could proclaim Jesus to their countrymen even if they didn't have the writings of John or Peter! They began with David, Isaiah, or even Moses. To the

Ethiopian official, Philip started with a passage in Isaiah 53 and proceeded to talk about Jesus (Acts 8:35). The Lord himself set the precedent for such preaching on the very day of His resurrection. "Beginning with Moses and all the Prophets, he explained to them what was said in all the Scriptures concerning himself" (Luke 24:27).

Old Testament—Reader's Digest Version

Luke records for us in Acts many examples of the early church's use of the Old Testament Scriptures. None is more illuminating than Stephen's defense address preserved in Acts 7. There Stephen provides a condensed version of two thousand years of Bible history. He divides this history into three great epochs and then concludes with a stinging rebuke of Hebrew faithlessness toward God. His theme through the entire discourse is this: Jehovah is the God of the universe. His acts and interests are not limited to one people or place. He demands obedience from all.

The faith of the fathers (7:2-16). Stephen begins with Abraham, the father of the Hebrew people. God called him to the land of promise. He gave the patriarch the "covenant of circumcision" and promised him a nation of descendants. Those descendants were not always faithful to God's plans. Joseph's brothers turned on him in jealousy and sold him into slavery. But God remained faithful to His promises despite the treachery of men.

Moses and the law (7:17-43). The patriarchs and their descendants eventually landed in slavery themselves. Still God was with them. He raised up Moses to deliver the nation from Egyptian bondage. But the people refused to obey Moses even after he had led them from Egypt. They turned to false gods and soon reaped the harvest of God's judgment. The prophets reminded the people of this many times.

The tabernacle and the temple (7:44-50). God not only gave the law to the Jews, which many disobeyed. He also gave them the "tabernacle of testimony" as a constant reminder of His presence with them. Later, Solomon built the temple as a house for God. But neither the tabernacle nor the temple was actually God's dwelling place. Isaiah said that no building made by man could contain God. Such was never God's purpose for these buildings.

Like father, like son (7:51-53). Stephen's conclusion is the strongest part of all. Those who opposed the messengers of the gospel were behaving exactly as their fathers had done before them. The fathers rejected the prophets, and their descendants killed the one the prophets predicted. Both the fathers and their descendants resisted the Holy Spirit, even as those who were listening to Stephen were doing. They had the law, but never obeyed it.

Portrait of a Spirit-filled man

Behind this powerful sermon stands Stephen the man. Luke first mentions him in Acts 6. The church selected him to aid the ministry to the Grecian widows. His qualifications for the position were impeccable.

First, he himself probably was a Grecian Jew, for his name is Greek rather than Hebrew. He and the other servants knew both the physical and the spiritual needs of their friends and neighbors in the church. Obviously Stephen was highly respected by those who knew him.

Second, Stephen was "full of the Spirit" (6:3). The Holy Spirit had full reign in his life, producing moral and spiritual maturity. The fruits of the Spirit abounded for all to see: "love, joy, peace, patience, kindness, goodness, faithfulness, gentleness, and self-control" (Galatians 5:22, 23).

He was also wise (6:3). In the Bible, the word *wisdom* describes a moral and spiritual quality, not just intellectual or academic achievement. A wise man understands God and His ways. He is able to discern between good and evil, and between what is best and what is merely good. Moreover, he can apply this spiritual knowledge to life.

Next, Stephen was full of faith (6:5). He trusted God not only in salvation, but with the daily issues of life as well. This combination of faith, wisdom, and spiritual maturity qualified him to be a man through whom God worked in special ways. Luke notes that Stephen, "a man full of God's grace and power, did great wonders and miraculous signs among the people" (6:8).

Stephen's encounter with the Jewish opposition reveals three other important qualities. He spoke with bold courage that comes only from the Lord. As Luke writes, "These men began to argue with Stephen, but they could not stand up against his wisdom or the Spirit by which he spoke" (6:9, 10). God was with him!

But in Stephen this boldness was mixed with innocence—a rare combination. To his opponents, his face was "like the face of an angel" (6:15). Few men can condemn the sins of others without letting their message become tainted with their own proud self-righteousness. Stephen had mastered that difficult assignment, and his message was therefore more powerful.

Even in Death

Most noticeably, Stephen displayed a superior ability to forgive. Only a man "full of the Spirit" could look his murderers in the eye and pray, "Lord, do not hold this sin against them" (7:60). He not only preached Jesus; he also died like Him!

In his novel entitled *The Robe*, Lloyd Douglas pictures Stephen at the moment of his death lifting his hand toward Heaven and shouting, "I see him! My Lord Jesus—take me!"

Marcellus, a character in Douglas's story, looks at a soldier standing nearby as the crowd melts away. Nervously, the soldier says Stephen thought someone was coming to rescue him. Marcellus replies confidently that Stephen did see someone coming.

"The dead Galilean, maybe?" ventures the soldier.

To that Marcellus replies, "That dead Galilean is not dead, my friend! He is more alive than any man here!"

And so was Stephen a moment later. How fitting that his name was Stephen, a Greek word meaning "crown"! Even before the Lord spoke the words recorded in Revelation, Stephen received the promise; "Be faithful, even to the point of death, and I will give you the crown of life" (Revelation 2:10).

The Trouble With Stephen

Of course, if we were to ask Stephen's opponents for their evaluation of the young Christian, we would get a completely different picture. He was a heretic and blasphemer! Officially, they charged him with speaking against the temple and the law. Actually, he had been preaching Jesus. He declared what Jesus had said, that His temple (His body) would be destroyed but raised again on the third day (John 2:19-21; Mark 14:58; Acts 6:13, 14). He taught that the Messiah's authority superseded even that of Moses and the law. Indeed, Jesus came to fulfill the law, not to destroy it.

Stephen's proclamation of Jesus was the real issue. He insisted that Jesus was the prophesied Messiah and that His countrymen had killed Him just as Jews of former generations had killed the prophets. Stephen referred to Jesus as the Son of Man (7:56). The hearers were Jews, and that term probably reminded them of Daniel's prophecy. Daniel spoke of one who would come from heaven to deliver His people (Daniel 7:13).

This Son of Man would be both deliverer of the righteous and judge of the unrighteous. The title was a clear sign of deity, something Stephen's opponents were unwilling to ascribe to Jesus.

Besides all this, Stephen took the very issue that the Jews were most proud of and turned it against them. You have received the law,'' he charged, ''but you have not obeyed it'' (7:53).

God's Strange Ways

God has a marvelous capacity for producing good even from the most evil events. So it was with Stephen's martyrdom. In the mob that condemned him was a young Pharisee named Saul. No one but God knew what was in store for him. Here he was a participant in the execution of a Christian preacher. Soon he would not only embrace the faith, but herald it across the empire.

VIII
Jonah: Act II
Acts 8–11

Everyone knows about Jonah, the guy who went fishing and became the catch instead of the catcher. But how many people really remember the lesson the Lord taught Jonah by his underwater adventure? Not many! In fact, even Peter, John, and a few others in the early church could have used a refresher course in Hebrew Prophets 301 at Jerusalem U.

Wrong Way Jonah

Jonah lived several hundred years before the time of Jesus. In his time Israel was surrounded by many powerful neighbors who threatened war at any time. One of the most awesome was Nineveh. Much to Jonah's surprise, Jehovah called him to preach repentance to, of all cities, Nineveh.

Jonah didn't mind preaching repentance as God directed, but to Nineveh? Perhaps he wouldn't even have minded visiting the Assyrian city to tell its people that God had decided to destroy them. But it seems the Lord wanted him to visit the pagan city and offer its people forgiveness if they would repent of their evil ways and believe God. That was asking too much!

The Lord ordered Jonah to Nineveh. But the prophet caught a ship at Joppa and headed toward Tarshish, in the opposite direction. That's when it happened! After a storm developed, the crew tossed Jonah overboard, hoping to appease God. Jonah was quickly swallowed by a huge fish especially prepared for the occasion by the Lord.

For three nightmarish days and nights, Jonah survived in the belly of the fish. In desperation he cried out to God for deliverance. He promised to do whatever the Lord told him. No matter what! The prophet of repentance himself repented. Finally the Lord spoke, and the fish cast Jonah out onto dry land.

Jonah Learns a Lesson

Again the Lord spoke to Jonah and sent him to Nineveh. This time he headed in the right direction. Once in the huge city he began proclaiming God's message. "In forty days," he told them, "the city will be destroyed unless you repent of your wicked ways." They actually believed him! A fast was proclaimed throughout the city as a sign of repentance. From the king to the lowliest citizen, everyone in the city dressed in sackcloth and ashes.

Jonah was angry! That was exactly what he was afraid would happen. He knew God had made a mistake. He had His opportunity to destroy the city outright. But no, He decided to give them another chance.

Still hoping that God might rain down fire and brimstone on the city, Jonah retreated a safe distance, made a shelter, and sat down to watch. While Jonah waited, God caused a large vine to sprout and grow over Jonah's shelter, providing much-appreciated shade. But almost immediately a worm began to eat the vine, causing it to wither and die. A hot wind arose, and the sun shone brighter than ever. Jonah collapsed from the scorching heat. Again in anger, he cried out to God.

This time God answered with a stern lesson for the reluctant prophet. "You had more compassion," the Lord scolded, "for that senseless vine than for a city full of people. If you can want a plant to live, why shouldn't I want to spare a city of a hundred thousand people!"

Jonah learned a lesson that day. God indeed is gracious, merciful, slow to anger, and abundant in lovingkindness (Jonah 4:2). He is not willing that any should perish, but that all should come to repentance, even Gentiles.

The Great Commission Army

The story of Jonah bears striking resemblance to the events of Acts 8—11. The Lord had given the church marching orders. "Go into all the world and preach the good news to all creation," He had said (Mark 16:15). "Go and make disciples of all nations" (Matthew 28:19). "This is what is written," he told them. "The Christ will suffer and rise from the dead on the third day, and repentance and forgiveness of sins will be preached in his name to all nations, beginning at Jerusalem" (Luke 24:46, 47). His parting words echoed the same message: "You will be my witnesses in Jerusalem, and in all Judea and Samaria, and to the ends of the earth" (Acts 1:8).

The Sons of Jonah

But note what the early church did. They preached the gospel all right. Thousands were saved. But as far as the written record of Acts is concerned, none of the apostles quickly made any effort to share the gospel with anyone except fellow Jews. At least five years passed before a single Gentile was ever baptized into Jesus (Acts 10), and many doubted whether that was proper or not. Probably another fifteen years passed before the question of Gentile Christians was completely settled (Acts 15).

Anywhere but Samaria

The first major outreach of the gospel beyond its Jewish beginnings was in Samaria. This province tucked between Galilee and Judea was a no man's land for orthodox Jews. Centuries before, the Samaritans had allowed both their race and their religion to become polluted by pagans. They were despised by their neighbors to the south and the north. In fact, a rigorous Jew would not even set foot on Samaritan soil if he could help it.

Jesus may have caused many an eyebrow to rise when He openly visited Samaritan villages, even talking with a woman of questionable reputation during a stop outside Sychar. In a parable, He cast a Samaritan in the role of hero, something no ordinary rabbi would have done. His last words to the disciples were plain: You are my witnesses—even in Samaria (Acts 1:8).

Yet no one went quickly to Samaria with the good news of Jesus. Finally Philip, a Greek-speaking Jew, found his way there when persecution forced the Christians out of Jerusalem. Samaria was undoubtedly a safe refuge. The Jerusalem rabbis might chase their opponents halfway around the world, but Samaria was off limits.

Once inside the safety of Samaria, Philip did not hide and wait for an opportunity to go home. He "bloomed where he was planted." He was surrounded by men and women who were lost, without God and without hope. So he did the most natural thing for an obedient disciple. He began to spread the message of Jesus. And many believed!

The Samaritan Problem

Philip's name is Greek instead of Hebrew. This leads us to suppose he was not a native of Palestine, but a foreign Jew who had come to Jerusalem for the feast of Pentecost and had become a Christian there. Now he was making Christians of Samaritans, large numbers of them.

Naturally this raised a question in the minds of the strict Jewish Christians who had lived in Judea all their lives and had been carefully taught to avoid Samaritans. Was it possible that God intended salvation for those half-heathen people as well as for His own chosen ones, the Jews?

There was a large possibility that another church might grow up in Samaria, believing in the same Christ, but preserving the ancient prejudice and having no fellowship with the church in Judea.

To the credit of the Christians in Jerusalem, they neither ignored the question nor decided it on the basis of their lifelong prejudice. They sent Peter and John to investigate.

The investigators found nothing out of order in Samaria. Philip was well known as a man "full of the Spirit and wisdom" (Acts 6:3). He preached the gospel truly, and God approved it with signs and wonders (Acts 8:6, 7). Many of the Samaritans sincerely believed and were baptized (Acts 8:12). All this was quite in accord with Jesus' parting instructions to the apostles (Acts 1:8). Peter and John added their approval to the approval God obviously was giving. They placed their hands on the Samaritans, who then received the Holy Spirit (Acts 8:17). The two apostles joined in preaching to the Samaritans, not only in the town where Philip was working, but in other villages as well (Acts 8:25).

Thereafter we read of "the church throughout Judea, Galilee, and Samaria" (Acts 9:31) as if there were no division. Among Christians the ancient enmity between Jews and Samaritans was no more.

All Men Are Kosher

The Samaritans' ancestry was mixed, partly Jewish and partly Gentile. The next major gospel breakthrough in Acts carried the good news of salvation into the Gentile world, to people who were not even partly Jewish. Peter again stood at center stage in God's drama of redemption. Years before, Jesus had promised that this big, husky fisherman would hold the keys to the kingdom of Heaven (Matthew 16:19). In Acts we read that Peter opened the door to each new group of believers. First he stood with the other apostles and spoke to the worldwide gathering of Jews at Pentecost (Acts 2). Later he went with John to assure the reception of Samaritan believers into the fellowship of the saved (Acts 8). Later still, he showed the way of salvation to Cornelius, a Gentile soldier (Acts 10). It seems that Cornelius and his associates were the first Gentiles to become Christians.

Like Jonah, Peter was anything but eager to share God's message of forgiveness with Gentile listeners. Jesus had sent the apostles to all the world (Mark 16:15), but none of them went to Gentiles till God acted again. In a vision, Peter was told that nothing God had cleansed was unclean. That was nothing new. Jesus had made all foods clean (Mark 7:19). But it was new to apply this principle to Gentiles.

Peter's lesson about kosher food was coupled with a visit from three messengers asking Peter to speak with their master. Peter obliged, and two days later he stood before Cornelius. But even then Peter failed to grasp the meaning of what was happening. Seeing a crowd of Gentiles gathered to meet him, he began by reminding them that coming there was something few Jews would do. He then asked what they wanted. Only when prompted did he begin to explain the message of Jesus.

Before he finished, God acted again! The Holy Spirit fell on the Gentiles as they listed to Peter's message. "The circumcised believers who had come with Peter was astonished that the gift of the Holy Spirit had been poured out even on the Gentiles. For they heard them speaking in tongues and praising God" (Acts 10:45, 46).

God's will was clear even to a preacher as reluctant as Jonah. "Can anyone keep these people from being baptized with water? They have received the Holy Spirit just as we have." So Peter ordered that they be baptized in the name of Jesus Christ (10:47, 48).

Even this didn't instantly settle the issue of Gentile evangelism for everybody. Peter was forced to explain his action to the other Jerusalem leaders (Acts 11). Later Paul would have to do the same thing (Acts 15). But the door was open. Cornelius was only the beginning.

IX
Faith Under Fire
Acts 12–14

It was Tertullian, the second-century Christian scholar, who first declared that ''the blood of the martyrs is the seed of the church.'' As a believer he knew what many enemies of the cross have since learned. Rather than destroying the church, persecution often only fans the flames of faith.

The Other Side of Faith

Though empowered by the Spirit, the church still faced adversity. Being a Spirit-filled church did not mean uninterrupted victory after victory. The early saints faced imprisonment, beatings, exile, and even death. Most remarkable of all, they looked upon such adversity with increased faith, not despair. God was giving them opportunities to show that His kingdom can withstand the worst that Satan has to offer.

The Rage of Hell

Opposition to the faith, past or present, is more than an idle accident of history. Such events are a part of a cosmic conspiracy, perpetuated in Hell itself. Satan's attacks on the young church began early in Acts. He started with threats. When the news of a lame man's healing and the apostles' proclamation of Christ reached the city authorities, Peter and John were seized and jailed (4:3). When warned to no longer speak in the name of Jesus, they boldly resisted. "We cannot help speaking about what we have seen and heard," they challenged (4:20).

The apostles' preaching continued. But so did the opposition. They were again jailed by the Sanhedrin, only to be miraculously released by the Lord. Once again they were arrested, and this time severely beaten (5:40).

First threats, next jail, and then beatings. Nothing stopped the stubborn preachers. One more step remained for Satan's servants—murder! Stephen, a vigorous and vocal Christian, was arrested on fabricated charges of blasphemy, dragged before the Jewish court, and finally stoned by an angry mob of vigilantes. Satan's last weapon—death—had been unleashed, but still the church grew, even more rapidly than before (6:8—7:60).

Saul of Tarsus soon became Satan's most valiant warrior. With unparalleled zeal he pursued the believers, dragging men and women alike to prison (8:3). Again Satan's plans were thwarted, in a most surprising way. The persecutor became a preacher! Surely Saul's conversion must have been the most startling news to reach the halls of Hell since the resurrection!

Despite Saul's loss, Satan continued his attacks against the church. James was killed, and Peter was again imprisoned (12:1-5). Eventually, Paul himself became the primary target of the persecution. From Jerusalem to Corinth, through all points in between, Paul's opponents followed him. But still he continued to proclaim the very message he once had hated.

A River of Blood

The first persecution of the church was a local matter, for the church itself was in only one locality. But gradually the trickle of blood became a scarlet torrent. In the imperial capital, Satan loosed his attacks with unlimited fury. First Nero and then one emperor after another sought to eliminate the Christians. It is thought that Peter and Paul were both victims of Nero's slaughter. Revelation was written against the background of the imperial persecution that plagued the church during the final decade of the first century.

But the worst persecution was still to come. During the second and third centuries thousands of believers were slaughtered. Many died in prison. Others fell by the sword. A few were crucified. In the darkest days Christians by the score were tossed to wild beasts in the Colosseum as thousands of cheering Romans watched the blood bath. But still they believed!

Why Me?

When persecution or a less violent form of adversity confronts the church, the faith of many believers is put to the test. Unfortunately not every Christian withstands the crisis with the same valor as the disciples in the early church. The faith of many falters at the earliest sign of difficulty. Perhaps the reason is the prevalence of distorted attitudes toward adversity and suffering.

Some contend that a truly Spirit-filled Christian need never face adversities or hardships. The Lord promises His disciples an abundant life—so the argument goes. For that life to be truly abundant it must be free of all suffering or pain. Needless to say, when a person who holds this position does confront a problem, his faith in the power and goodness of God is called into question. The reality of his plight soon leads to deadly doubt or paralyzing guilt.

Similarly, others consider all adversity as divine punishment. Like Job's friends, such disciples insist that a good man would never suffer affliction. If adversity does come it is evidence of sin. Such thinking created serious problems for many first-century Christians who had converted from Judaism. When persecution developed, some immediately considered their plight a sign of God's disfavor with their decision to trust Jesus. The Hebrew Epistle was penned, in part, to remind such troubled believers of the importance of keeping the faith even in the face of adversity.

Such misunderstandings of adversity frequently lead to a practical consequence. Peace, prosperity, and success become the measure of faithfulness. Convinced of this, the believer develops a willingness to do anything that promises to minimize difficulties. Courage, sacrifice, and endurance have no meaning for such disciples.

The Call to Courage

If such attitudes had dominated the life of the church in Acts, the gospel would have never gone beyond the walls of the upper room. But Peter, John, Stephen, and the rest maintained a completely different view of adversity. They didn't want it, but neither did they consider suffering as a sign of God's judgment or the sufferer's faithlessness. Peace and prosperity appealed to them just as much as to any modern believer. But there were other issues of life more important than personal comfort. Some things were worth suffering for!

Because these early Christians were followers of Jesus, they expected adversity. "A student is not above his teacher, nor a servant above his master," Jesus had warned them (Matthew 10:24). "If they persecuted me, they will persecute you also" (John 15:20). "Dear friends," Peter later wrote, "do not be surprised at the painful trial you are suffering, as though something strange were happening to you. But rejoice that you participate in Christ's sufferings, so that you may be overjoyed when his glory is revealed" (1 Peter 4:12, 13).

The early Christians also knew that adversity can sometimes actually be beneficial. James testified of this when he wrote, "Consider it pure joy, my brothers, whenever you face trials of many kinds, because you know that the testing of your faith develops perseverance. Perseverence must finish its work so that you may be mature and complete, not lacking anything" (James 1:2-4).

As unlikely as it must have seemed at the time, the persecutions inflicted upon the early church actually resulted in good. Forced to flee their homes, the first-century saints headed for other towns and villages throughout the empire, taking with them the gospel. Even Stephen's death must have played an important role in the conversion of Saul, who later heralded the gospel in places Stephen would not have gone and with effectiveness that Stephen could have never matched. Augustine was once asked why the Lord allowed Stephen to suffer so. He answered that God had chosen to work His redemptive plan within the confines of human nature. "If Stephen had not spoken thus, if he had not prayed thus, the church would not have had Paul," he insisted.

Adversity often provides opportunity for faith, opportunity that the believer eagerly anticipates. When the apostles were beaten for preaching, they didn't despair. They rejoiced "because they had been counted worthy of suffering disgrace for the Name" (Acts 5:41). Paul demonstrated the same eagerness to put his faith into practice against adversity. Even though warned by a prophet of God that prison and hardship awaited him if he went to Jerusalem, he none the less persisted. "However, I consider my life worth nothing to me, if only I may finish the race and complete the task the Lord Jesus has given me—the task of testifying to the gospel -of God's grace" (Acts 20:24).

And James Died!

Acts 12 contains an interesting sidelight into the reality of suffering and adversity. King Herod arrested some church leaders, Peter and James among them. Both were men of God; both were important leaders in the Jerusalem church. But only Peter, not James, was miraculously rescued. James the brother of John was put to death by the sword.

God doesn't always rescue His saints. Sometimes they suffer and even die! And no one knows in advance who must suffer and who will be spared. Nor do we know the reasons. That was essentially God's message to Job in the Old Testament. Man simply doesn't always know the mind of God. Sometimes He calls us to walk through the fire. Yet even then He stands with us in adversity, not just apart from it!

The saints in Acts also had a mature view of joy. They knew that joy and happiness can never be limited to externals. Joy comes from the inside. Because of this Paul and Silas could sing even in jail. "Rejoice in the Lord always. I will say it again," declared Paul: "Rejoice!" "I have learned to be content whatever the circumstances. I know what it is to be in need, and I know what it is to have plenty. I have learned the secret of being content in any and every situation, whether well-fed or hungry, whether living in plenty or in want. I can do everything through Him who gives me strength" (Philippians 4:4, 11-13).

A second-century historian spoke of the overwhelming joy of the early Christians when he wrote, "These Christians are a strange lot. They follow their dead, singing the Psalms and acting as though this was a time of joy and jubilation. They are undaunted by any defeat, even the defeat of death."

How to Handle Hardship

What did the early church do when the going got tough? Give up? Never! Compromise their faith? Absolutely not! Nor did they simply wait quietly and do nothing. Instead they did the only two things than any believer can do when confronted with overwhelming obstacles.

First, they reaffirmed their faith in God. That's what Paul and Silas were doing in the Philippian jail (Acts 16:25). They sang hymns. They joyously lifted their voices in glory to God. Satan can handle almost any response to his attacks except Spirit-filled praise. Arguments, verbal attacks, anger—none of these deter the tempter. But when one of God's children turns to the Father in open praise, Satan knows that his defeat is certain.

The other response of a faithful church to adversity is prayer—not just mouthing pious words, but turning to God fully expecting Him to act. When Peter was imprisoned again and possibly headed for the same fate as James, the church acted in faith. They gathered in prayer, beseeching the God of Heaven to act in their behalf. And act He did, even sooner and more decisively than they expected (Acts 12:12-17).

The same God rules the world today. And today prayer and praise still are the disciples' most effective weapons against Satan's battle plans.

X
When Christians Disagree
Acts 15

Consider the plight of the church building committee that was meeting in their new basement because there were no lights in the church auditorium. One committee member made a motion that the church purchase a chandelier for the upstairs. An older man on the committee objected vigorously. He listed his reasons. "First," he said, "no one can play it. Second, we can't afford it; and third, what we need is lights!"

Funny? Yes, indeed. But many Christians must laugh at such stories to keep from crying. They've seen too many churches split wide open over situations just as ridiculous.

Grown men and women have refused to speak to each other for years because of disagreements long since forgotten by both. Congregations have divided over who plays the piano, where the choir stands, or what color to paint the parsonage. One church was kept in a constant state of confusion by two leaders who would almost come to blows over the temperature at which to set the thermostat.

Destructive Division

Do such problems really matter? Yes indeed! They matter because they destroy the thing Jesus prayed for in His church—unity. "I pray . . . that all of them may be one, Father," said the Savior, "just as you are in me and I am in you. May they also be in us so that the world may believe that you have sent me" (John 17:20, 21).

Jesus placed unity high on His priority list for His followers. He knew a divided church is poor advertisement. A lost world already filled with strife and hatred will very seldom take seriously a church that fails to practice what it preaches.

The Make-believe Church

Imagine how wonderful it would be to live in an age in which Christians never disagreed, never quarrelled, and never divided over the petty issues of opinion. Before you drift off into "never-never-land" dreaming of such golden days, take another look at the church in the New Testament. Despite popular myths to the contrary, divided churches are not a modern invention. The first century had more than its share. Interpersonal problems, leadership disputes, division over spiritual gifts, doctrinal quarrels, sectarianism, party politics—these and almost every other problem you name can be found in the New Testament.

Problems, Problems

A closer look at the church in Acts uncovers some of the sticky disagreements that threatened to derail the new faith before it even got going. The first was an ethnic problem (Acts 6:1-7). For the first decade of its life, the church was composed almost completely of Jews. But among those Jews were two distinct groups, Hebrews and Grecian Jews. The first lived in Palestine, and their native language was Hebrew, or

Aramaic, as some prefer to call the speech of the Hebrews at that time. The Grecian Jews lived in other countries. They spoke the native languages of those countries. Most of them also spoke Greek, for before the time of Christ the conquests of Alexander the Great had spread that language through the Mediterranean world. Many of these Grecian Jews became Christians on the Day of Pentecost, and then stayed in Jerusalem instead of going back home.

Not long after Pentecost, a dispute arose within the Christian community. For whatever reason, some of the Grecian Jews came to believe that widows among them were being overlooked in the benevolent ministry of the church. The dispute was brought to the apostles and quickly defused.

The second major problem noted in Acts may be called a racial matter. However, it was entwined with a very knotty doctrinal issue and involved strong emotions. This second disagreement began to develop as more and more Gentiles came to accept the gospel. Some Jewish Christians questioned the propriety of allowing Gentiles full membership in the church without requiring them to submit to the dictates of the Jewish law. In other words, could a Gentile become a Christian without also becoming a Jew?

That was no small problem for the first-century church. The solution to that issue would affect the future of the church for generations to come. So serious was the problem that a major gathering of church leaders was called to consider it (Acts 15:1-35). This disagreement also was solved, to the joy of Christians everywhere.

A third disagreement recorded by Luke was of a personal nature. It involved Paul and Barnabas, two missionary partners, and a third co-worker, John Mark (Acts 15:36-41). As Paul and Barnabas prepared for another evangelistic tour, Barnabas suggested taking

71

John Mark with them. Paul objected because the young worker had abandoned them in the middle of a previous journey. Barnabas was willing to give him another chance. The problem became so severe that the two long-time co-workers agreed to disagree. They went their separate ways, Barnabas taking John Mark and Silas accompanying Paul.

Putting Out the Fire

Sometimes even the most spiritual church encounters difficulties that threaten its unity. Acts documents that fact quite clearly. The secret of spiritual vitality is not the absence of disagreements, but the ability to handle differences in wise and constructive ways.

The early church's discussion of the Gentile question (Acts 15:1-35) provides a classic case study on how to handle a potentially divisive issue. As noted before, this was an emotional issue. Many in the church had already chosen sides and were prepared for battle. Yet despite this, the church maintained its unity. How did they do it? Consider the following factors.

Facing the Problem

First, they faced the problem openly. When Judean brethren began teaching the law, Paul and Barnabas didn't remain silent. Nor did they simply protest to each other about the problem. They went directly to the source of the mistaken teaching and disputed the issue with the teachers themselves.

True unity is never preserved by pretending a disagreement doesn't exist. Open, honest discussion is essential. But the worst possible course of action is to talk about the problem to everyone but those directly involved. Paul, Barnabas, and apparently those on the other side of the question cared enough about unity to talk with each other face to face. Jesus encouraged this approach to interpersonal problems when He told His disciples to take up a problem personally with the brother involved (Matthew 5:23-26; 18:15-20).

Learning to Listen

Second, when the two sides were unable to resolve the problem between themselves, they consented to submit it to another authority. In this case, they appealed to the elders and apostles at Jerusalem. The first preachers of the gospel were there, and they should be able to determine which faction at Antioch was preaching it truly. Seeking such counsel indicates how much the people at Antioch wanted the problem solved. Lesser men might have resisted such a suggestion. "We know we're right! Why bother somebody else?" they could have argued.

Apparently both sides went to Jerusalem with a willingness to accept the verdict, whatever it might be. More than they wanted a decision in their favor, they wanted the truth established and the fellowship of the church preserved.

At the Jerusalem meeting, as at Antioch, open debate dominated the scene. There were no back-room bargains, no political maneuvering such as sometimes affects even religious discussions. Everyone was treated in an open and honest way. Paul and Barnabas were completely willing to let the other side speak, and the other side let Paul and Barnabas have their say. Those devoted to truth need not fear open discussion.

Not only did both sides speak openly, but they also listened to each other. In the midst of disagreements, the listening is often more important than the talking. As James, a prominent speaker in the Jerusalem meeting, later phrased it, "Everyone should be quick to listen, slow to speak, and slow to become angry" (James 1:19).

73

Focusing on God

Next, notice that the discussion in Acts 15 centered on the things God had been doing in the church. Both Paul and Peter recounted how the Lord had opened the way to Gentile evangelism. A God-centered rather than a man-centered approach to Christian discussion paves the way to lasting unity. When men focus their attention on what they have accomplished rather than on the power of God, walls of division grow taller.

This God-centeredness led the believers to consider their problem and potential decision in the proper context. The question was not "How can I win the argument?" It was "How can God's plan for the church be followed?" Once they had established the principle that the Lord wanted His church to herald the gospel to *all* men, their next decision seemed more obvious.

The twentieth-century church can follow this example. "What is God's primary concern for the church?" This is properly the first question. Once the church realizes that God wants His followers to turn the world right side up by living the Christian life and preaching the gospel to all, the color of the carpet, the setting of the thermostat, or any other petty problem is seen in a new light.

A Word From the Word

Another vital part of the church's decision-making procedure was the Scriptures. Note the speeches and decisions of the Jerusalem meeting. The Scriptures were referred to, quoted, and accepted as the authoritative voice on the subject. From the Scriptures the church learned God's priorities and plans for His people. Clearly, even a spirit-filled, charismatic, apostolic church required the guidance of the written Word.

Spirit-led Decisions

The church in Acts also sought the Holy Spirit's guidance in its decisions. The Christians preceded each decision with prayer. In Acts 1, they selected Judas' replacement in a way that put the final decision in God's hands. The church believed without reservation that the Lord had a stake in the decision and that He wanted to be heard!

When the Jerusalem conference reached its conclusion, credit was given to the Holy Spirit. "It seemed good to the Holy Spirit and to us," the apostles and elders wrote.

Once the decision was reached, the apostles and elders made the matter public. A letter was drafted and sent to all concerned churches.

Finally, the Christians followed through by doing what they said they would do. Nothing frustrates unity in the fellowship faster than inconsistency and unfulfilled promises.

The Good Side of Disagreements

Are disagreements between fellow believers always bad? Not necessarily. Harm may be turned aside if problems can be resolved in the proper way. In fact, occasional disagreements can be a sign of health. They mean that the members of the fellowship are thinking, caring persons. Apathy may sometimes be disguised as unity, but there is a world of difference between the two.

XI
How to Win the World
Acts 13, 14, 16, 17

God leaves the church in the world for one reason—to grow, to win more and more people to Jesus! If He has another purpose for His people, He could accomplish it better by taking us to Heaven the moment we are born again into the kingdom. Fellowship, worship, and personal learning could all be done better in Heaven than on earth. But there is one kingdom task that can be done only on earth—sharing the Christ with the lost! If the world is to hear the gospel, it will hear because the church is busy about the Father's business.

The Holy Growth in Acts

One of the most striking facts about the church in Acts is its explosive growth. Only about one hundred twenty believers were with the apostles before Pentecost (Acts 1:15). But in just one day, three thousand new believers embraced Jesus Christ (2:41). Before long, there were over five thousand Christian *men* in Jerusalem (4:4). Soon the church increased so rapidly that Luke no longer wrote that numbers were *added* to the church. Instead, he said they *multiplied* (6:1, 7; 9:31, King James Version).

The expansion of the faith didn't stop in Jerusalem. As the Lord had commanded, the church set its sights on the world. Within a generation, whole regions were hearing the gospel (Acts 19:10). Paul could even write of its impact "all over the world" (Colossians 1:6).

Is it still possible for the church to have the same extraordinary impact on the world? Yes, indeed. The same Lord rules from Heaven. Our message is the same! And lost men still thirst for the water of life.

The big question is "how?" How did the first-century church manage to spread the gospel so rapidly? How can our churches restore that fact of New Testament life today? Luke records many ingredients that fueled the evangelistic fire of the early church. Let's consider a few of these principles as illustrated in the missionary methods of Paul and his co-workers.

Spirit-led Evangelism (Acts 13:1-3)

The most important factor in the church's growth was the Holy Spirit. The New Testament insists that winning the world is a cooperative effort involving both God and His chosen servants (1 Corinthians 3:5-9). In Acts we see that the Spirit guided the church's choice of messengers, closed and opened doors for witness, opened the hearts of hearers, and created opportunities for preaching. Today as then, the first step toward winning the world is to let the Spirit rather than man program our ministries. It can happen!

Second, Luke describes congregational evangelism. At the Holy Spirit's direction, Paul's first missionary journey was initiated and financed by the Antioch Christians. That local congregation assumed responsibility for spreading the gospel not only in its own community, but in much wider areas. Later Paul and Barnabas reported back to that church concerning the results of their journey. Today as well, effective evangelism begins in congregations. Seminaries, evangelistic societies, mission boards, and other para-church groups can have a vital impact on the lost world, but only to the degree that congregations of concerned believers empower them to do evangelistic work.

The early church also knew the benefits of teamwork. Jesus set the example when He sent the twelve and later the seventy two by two (Mark 6:7-13; Luke 10:1-12). After Jesus was gone, the disciples continued to work in teams. Paul and Barnabas, and later Paul and Silas, traveled together, along with Timothy, Luke, and others. Each contributed his unique abilities and gifts to the kingdom effort, supplementing and complementing the skills of his co-workers. Such team work is actually a form of the body life described in Romans 12:3-8. No one, not even an apostle Paul, can by himself do all God wants done. He needs other members of the body to minister to him and to multiply his efforts.

Telling It Like It Is (Acts 13:6-12)

Paul's most basic evangelistic method was verbal—the bold, uncompromising proclamation of the gospel. "How, then, can they call on the one they have not believed in? And how can they believe in the one of whom they have not heard? And how can they hear without someone preaching to them? . . . Faith comes from hearing the message, and the message is heard through the word of Christ," Paul wrote (Romans 10:14, 17). He was not content to witness passively through his "good life." He took the offensive, confronting evil and proclaiming Christ wherever he had the opportunity.

Starting at Home Plate (Acts 13:4, 5, 13-15; 14:1)

No baseball player ever scored a run by beginning at second base. He always starts from home. Likewise, Paul knew evangelism doesn't start by "winning the world." It starts with a few individuals with whom one has a natural contact. At times Paul went to the market place and preached to anyone who would listen. But more often he sought out groups of Jewish people with whom e already had a great deal in common. Once he had established a nucleus of disciples, he would branch out to others and begin to work with them.

Paul always went to where the people were. He didn't set up shop in a secluded church house and wait for the world to find him. He went to the major cities to preach. Antioch, Derbe, Lystra, Ephesus, Philippi, Corinth, Athens—his itinerary reads like a list of the biggest cities of the Roman Empire. He knew that these cities not only were home to thousands but also affected the lives of many others through their influence on commerce, education, and politics. Choosing these cities rather than others was a matter of stewardship of time and resources.

Paul went to the cities to seek out people. He went to the synagogues, market places, and even from house to house preaching the gospel. His was a people-oriented ministry.

In a way, Paul's concern for people affected what he preached as well as where he preached it. Compare his message to the Jewish audience at Pisidian Antioch (Acts 13:14-41) with his sermon at Athens (17:22-31). In each case he geared the gospel to the audience. For the synagogue crowd, he began with Moses and the law. From there he proceeded to the gospel. The pagan philosophers knew little of the Old Testament. For them, he started with their religion, but quickly worked his way to Jesus.

Preaching Christ and Him Crucified (Acts 13:26-30)

Wherever Paul preached or at whatever point he began, he always preached Jesus and the resurrection. He didn't labor over petty doctrinal issues or human religious traditions. He simply pointed men to Jesus. In that message, and that message alone, was power to convict men of sin and change lives. Time hasn't changed that fact!

Making Disciples That Last (Acts 14:22, 23)

Paul's task wasn't complete when he preached Jesus and men responded. He assumed personal responsibility for their growth in the faith. In short, his goal was self-reproducing disciples, not just quick converts. Sometimes he stayed in a city for a long time in order to teach the new believers. Often he returned to a city to see how the disciples were doing. But perhaps most importantly, Paul planted churches. He brought believers together to form congregations. He helped develop spiritual leadership for the congregations so the new disciples would continue in the faith long after he was gone.

Effective follow-up is one of the most difficult parts of evangelism, but one of the most important. Perhaps that's why Jesus' commission commands disciple-making and teaching rather than just winsome preaching. Disciple-making and church-planting may take longer, but the results are far more lasting and far reaching.

All Things To All Men (Acts 16:3)

Another important part of Paul's evangelistic strategy was his "all things to all men" attitude. He wrote of this to the Corinthians: "Though I am free and belong to no man, I make myself a slave to everyone, to win as many as possible. To the Jews I became like a Jew, to win the Jews. To those under the law I became like one under the law (though I myself am not under the law), so as to win those under the law. To those not having the law I became like one not having the law (though I am not free from God's law but am under Christ's law), so as to win those not having the law. To the weak I became weak, to win the weak. I have become all things to all men so that by all possible means I might save some. I do all this for the sake of the gospel that I may share in its blessings" (1 Corinthians 9:19-23).

Paul is not talking about spinelessly compromising his message and life to impress his hearers. Not at all! He's talking about self-sacrifice, the willingness to forego personal rights for the sake of others. He practiced this himself. And he encouraged his co-workers to do the same.

Blooming Where You're Planted (Acts 16:25)

Paul's concern for the lost was not just a professional strategy. It was personal conviction. He shared Jesus wherever he was, in jail as well as in church. Especially enlightening is what Paul did when his plans were interrupted. When he arrived in Athens, he had planned to wait for Silas and Timothy so they could begin their next evangelistic campaign together. But waiting in idleness was one thing Paul couldn't do, at least not when a lost city lay at his doorstep. First in the synagogue, and then in the market place, Paul began preaching, not because Athens was the next city on his crusade schedule, but because he was there! (Acts 17:15-17).

Too Good to Keep

Have you ever heard someone tell you a bit of news that you knew others were eager to hear? If so, you know the feeling of knowing something too good to keep to yourself. It seems you'll almost burst before you get the message out. That attitude is the key to winning our world for Christ. That's what kept Paul going. That's also what motivated untold thousands of early Christians to share their faith with everyone they came in contact with.

Celsus, one of the bitterest enemies of the faith in the second century, offered a striking commentary on the evangelistic zeal of the Christians. In his writings he ridiculed the believers for being mainly uneducated people such as weavers, cobblers, laundry workers, and farm laborers. But he went on to complain that one had only to look the other way for a Christian to turn up and try to spread his propaganda.

Winning the world! An impossible task? In a sense it is impossible. We know that the whole world will never accept the gospel. But on the other hand, we don't know who will and who won't accept. Our target therefore must be all men. We dare not aim lower.

XII
God's Little People
Acts 18–20

Bill is an average guy. He is neither tall nor short, just average. In school, he never fails a course. But neither does he do especially well. He is—average! In sports, music, romance, you name it, Bill is an average guy.

Bill is also a Christian, which in itself makes him a bit non-average when compared to his fellow university students. But Bill does have a problem. You might call it a spiritual inferiority complex. He really wants to serve the Lord. More than anything else in the world, Bill wants to make his life count for Christ. But he is convinced that there is nothing he can ever do that God can use.

"I'm just average. How can God use me?" he laments.

A World of Little People

Bill is a fictitious person—in a sense. I really didn't have any one person in mind as I described him. I was thinking of *many* people. In fact, the world is full of

Bills, people who are convinced that God is only interested in the "superstars." The Bills in the church are the devoted believers who labor in the shadows, never quite realizing that what they do can be just as important as the exploits of those in the limelight.

It is easy to understand how many of us develop such attitudes. We read the Bible and learn of Abraham, David, Peter, Paul, and other famous men who lived extraordinary lives. When we read church history or look around at history in the making, all we ever hear about are the rich, the famous, the very bright, or the very talented. If we happen to be just average, we soon conclude that God uses only the exceptional.

The Saints Behind the Scenes

How wrong can we be! God does have His "superstars," but they are few and far between. Most of the time God uses "little people" who have big faith. In fact, Paul suggests that if some abilities or spiritual gifts are more favored by God, they are those less favored by man (1 Corinthians 12:21-25).

In his book *Full Circle,* David R. Mains offers a comment that every Bill in the church needs to hear. He says every true church member has at least one gift or talent. Most people have more than one, but no one has all the gifts needed in the work of the church. Members of the church therefore are interdependent, for everyone has something to contribute and everyone lacks something that others can supply. First Corinthians 12:21-25 indicates that some gifts are less spectacular, but not less necessary. "The church can go a long time without a miracle," says Mr. Mains, "but let it try to exist without acts of mercy or contributions!"

Consider the early church, for example. Acts has only a few big names. In fact, most of Luke's record deals with two men, Peter and Paul. But they weren't the only Spirit-powered men. There were countless others whose names we never think to suggest for God's great Hall of Faith, but who nevertheless were the backbone of the church. Bill and the rest of us who'll never be a Peter or Paul can learn a lot by just remembering the lives of some of the lesser-known saints.

Barnabas—Son of Encouragememt

Barnabas is one of those lesser names in Acts without whom the story of the early church might never have been written. His real name was Joseph, but quickly his Christian associates gave him a new name. They called him "son of encouragement." He had the God-given ability to comfort, encourage, and exhort other brothers.

I think of Barnabas as a coach. A great athlete doesn't necessarily make a great coach. The coach needs the ability to play the game, but more than that he must be able to draw the best out of others. He must teach, motivate, cheer, and then stay on the sidelines while others play the game.

Barnabas was first of all a giver. Along with others, he sold property and brought the money to the apostles for distribution among the needy believers (Acts 4:36, 37). His example stands in direct contrast to the action of Ananias and Sapphira (5:1-11). They wanted more recognition than they deserved. Barnabas simply wanted to help. He gave because he cared.

He also had the capacity to reach out and forgive when others wouldn't. When Paul began preaching the gospel, who was it that stood up for him when no one else would trust him? Who else but Barnabas! (9:27). When suspicions were running rampant in the Jerusalem church about the activities in Antioch, whom did the apostles trust to investigate the situation and bring back a fair report? Barnabas again!

(11:19-24). Who not only accepted Paul but recruited him as a co-worker? Who else but Barnabas? (11:25, 26). Who even stood up to Paul in order to give young John Mark a second chance? Barnabas—the son of encouragement! (15:36-41).

How desperately the church needs encouragers—men who will live for others, men like Barnabas who can give, forgive, and keep on forgiving and giving when lesser men have stopped! Such men seldom get the honor they deserve—at least not in this world. Some day even that will change!

Aquila and Priscilla—a Model Marriage

Luke seldom mentions the families of the church, but one family that he does mention provides a classic example of how the Lord uses the home as an instrument of faith.

From the description, Aquila and Priscilla must have made a fine team. They were co-workers—"one flesh" in the fullest sense of the term. They worked together, prayed together, and taught together. They were a couple, two people whom God had joined together, not separate individuals who just shared the same house. A justice of the peace can join two people in marriage, but only God can create a spiritual partnership like that of Aquila and Priscilla.

Together Mr. and Mrs. Aquila demonstrated the gift of hospitality. When Paul came to Corinth, they opened their home to him (Acts 18:1-4). Later they moved to Ephesus, and when Apollos came to town, he too visited their home. Together Aquila and Priscilla took the young preacher under their wings and carefully taught him the way of God more completely (18:24-26). Later still, in another city, their home became a meeting place for the church (Romans 16:3-5).

Hospitality is not just a matter of entertaining strangers. A warm meal and soft bed are only the start.

True hospitality is a spiritual ministry. A home turned over to the Lord becomes a place of great influence. People who would never enter a church building will often eagerly listen to the gospel in the shelter of a friendly home. Men like Apollos who might otherwise resist correction melt before the quiet teaching of a family that has first given friendship.

Apollos—a Teacher Who Was Taught

Little is known about Apollos, but what information there is is impressive. Coming from Alexandria, the chief Jewish educational center outside of Jerusalem, he was a learned man. Luke describes him as "mighty in the Scriptures" (Acts 18:24, King James Version). Moreover, he was a gifted preacher. When he spoke men listened. Yet there was a problem. He knew the basic facts about Jesus, but apparently had never had the full gospel explained to him. Luke doesn't go into detail about Apollos's doctrinal problem, but apparently he lacked an understanding of Christian baptism and of the ministry of the Holy Spirit.

What did the young scholar do when confronted with his misunderstanding? Not many bright young theologians would have paid much attention to an ordinary tentmaker and his wife. What did they know? Had they ever gone to the seminary in Alexandria? But Apollos was wise beyond his learning. He had a teachable spirit!

Because Apollos was so gifted, men naturally followed him. Paul noted that one of the divisions in the Corinthian church centered around him (1 Corinthians 3:4-7). Apollos could have encouraged his followers and built up a sect devoted to him. But he didn't. Apollos was not a selfish empire builder. Later he refused to return to Corinth when Paul urged him to go (1 Corinthians 16:12). The reason may have been that he did not want to strengthen any inclination to follow him. He wanted the church built up in unity more than he wanted his own reputation and following enlarged.

Men With a Mission

Some of the real "superstars" of the early church are never named by Luke. These were not Peter or Paul or Apollos, but the local leaders of the faith, the pastors and shepherds of the flocks, the men who personally assumed the spiritual responsibility of the churches. We do not know their names, but we owe these men a great debt.

Luke does preserve a mini-portrait of such leaders in Paul's farewell address to the Ephesian elders (Acts 20:17-35). These leaders had two main objectives: 1) to live the Christian life themselves and 2) to aid their flock in spiritual growth (20:28). They were not professional workers who performed a job without personal involvement. Their first task was to walk what they talked.

Paul emphasizes this principle in his discussion of church leaders in 1 Timothy 3 and Titus 1. Almost every item on Paul's list of qualifications for elders relates to character, not talent. His concern was that church leaders first be men worthy of leadership. They were to be men who could lead others in discipleship because they were living what they taught.

The specific duties of these leaders flow quite naturally from the quality of their personal lives. First they were to feed the church (Acts 20:28, King James Version). The New International Version says, "Be shepherds of the church." That is a good way to put it, for the word translated "feed" means more than that. It includes all the care, guidance, and protection a shepherd gives his sheep. The elders were to care for the church in the same ways. They were shepherds who could show the flock where to find food and water because they had already been there.

Next, the elders were to guard against false teachers (20:29-31). Exposing wolves was a sad task, but necessary. The wise and good elders could detect the false only because they recognized the true.

Also, the elders were to rely on the word of God's grace (20:32). Their ability to keep the faith and to guard the flock would come from God. The moment they started relying on their own strength they would fail. They were God's men, not their own. They needed to treasure God's Word, live by it, and teach it.

Finally, they must demonstrate a servant's spirit. Giving, not taking or demanding, was their task. If a man wanted a position of power or authority, the role of a shepherd was not for him. The pastor was first a servant who taught others how to serve (20:33-35).

The Men God Uses

God uses *people* to accomplish His perfect will. He uses all kinds of people, but mostly He uses those whose attitude makes them useable. Availability, not ability, is the key. He provides the gifts and talents needed to do His work, but usually His work is done through those who are willing to be used.

XIII
Jesus for President!
Acts 21–28

Balancing faithfulness to God and loyalty to country has sometimes been difficult for Christians. The believers in Acts faced the problem almost immediately. Today many of the issues have changed, at least for those of us who live in the free world. But there is still the same need for Christians to clearly understand the relationship of their faith to their country. Even in the more or less democratic nations, some believers are confronted with the temptation to deify their rulers and make the state the supreme authority in life. In fact, nationalism may well be the most prevalent form of idolatry today. On the other hand, some Christians are tempted to defy their government, to resist even with violence when a law is not to their liking.

Empowered by the Holy Spirit, the church in Acts faced the challenge of the government. What they did and how they did it provides valuable lessons for Christians of all time. They did not resort to violence and neither did they allow the government to take the place of God.

The Law Above the Law

Throughout the early years of the faith, Christians were confronted with the issue of political obedience in a very practical way. The church could assemble, sing, pray, and do many other "religious" activities. But they were told to keep the gospel to themselves. Many modern believers would find it easy to obey such an order. But not the saints of Acts. Jesus had said "preach the gospel to every creature" (Mark 16:15, King James Version). So preach they must, whether the local politicians liked it or not (Acts 5:27-29, 40-42).

Why did they persist even though it meant disobeying a legitimate government authority? Because they were convinced that they were ruled by an even higher authority—the Creator himself! Jesus was their King, their President! If they had a choice they would obey their human rulers, but in this case they felt compelled to follow Jesus. Peter and John explained, "Judge for yourselves whether it is right in God's sight to obey you rather than God. For we cannot help speaking about what we have seen and heard" (Acts 4:19, 20).

But note, these believers did not disobey the law simply for the sake of personal convenience or because they didn't like the ordinance. The gospel was at stake. They were willing to place their lives on the line to share the good news with others. Whenever the Spirit leads a man to disobey the law it is always for others, not self!

An Attitude of Submission

Also involved in the early Christian response to the political powers was an attitude of submission. They actually believed that God could use even the most corrupt leaders to maintain peace and justice. In Paul's words, "The authorities that exist have been established by God. Consequently, he who rebels against the authority is rebelling against what God has instituted" (Romans 13:1, 2).

At times the Christians were forced to disobey even what they felt was a God-established authority. But even then they did so in a submissive manner. Peter and John disobeyed the order to stop preaching, and immediately they were arrested and beaten. But not once did they resist, attempt to break out of jail by force, or in any other way incite to violence. They disobeyed the official orders when they had to, but when they disobeyed they accepted the consequences without rebellion.

Later when Paul was arrested on false charges he even apologized for his disrespectful words to the high priest before whom he was charged. When confronted with his actions, he replied, "Brothers, I did not realize that he was the high priest; for it is written: 'Do not speak evil about the ruler of your people' " (Acts 23:5).

Why this sensitivity to a rebellious spirit? Because Paul, Peter, and the others knew that rebellion is contagious. Worse yet, rebellious people are seldom attentive to the claims of Christ. The best chance that most men have for hearing the gospel comes in an environment of peace. Paul encouraged his fellow Christians "that requests, prayers, intercession, and thanksgiving be made for everyone—for kings and all those in authority, that we may live peaceful and quiet lives in all godliness and holiness. This is good, and pleases God our Savior, who wants all men to be saved and come to a knowledge of the truth" (1 Timothy 2:1-4).

The Courage to Care

Paul illustrated another important attitude toward "the powers that be." When arrested and placed on trial before the king, he used that very opportunity to share Christ. He wasn't intimidated by the throne. He courageously proclaimed the same message to the king that he did to the beggar. Before Agrippa, the apostle openly declared his zeal to evangelize even the king himself (Acts 26:29).

Paul's boldness was demonstrated also in his message to Felix. His preaching of "righteousness, self-control, and the judgment to come" was so to the point that Felix's heart was flooded with fear. A lesser man might have spoken in vague generalities, but not Paul. He directed his words to the very center of the ruler's sin-saturated life (Acts 24:24, 25).

Declaring the good news of Jesus requires true boldness. Whether before world rulers, next-door neighbors, or dear friends, the disciple must be "speaking the truth in love" (Ephesians 4:15).

The Practice of Freedom

Paul also demonstrated how a Christian can use political freedom for kingdom purposes. More than once when arrested, Paul claimed his rights as a Roman citizen (Acts 16:37; 22:22-29). Each time the freedom that was his as a citizen not only protected his life, but also opened new doors of witness.

In a free society, the privileges of citizenship become a Christian's responsibility. The right to vote, to campaign, to protest—in short, all the rights of citizenship are tools to bring about godly change in a godless society.

The God Who Rules

Perhaps the most important attitude of all in the early Christians' response to the political powers was the deep-seated conviction that God is the real ruler of the world. They actually believed that the sovereign God of the universe was ultimately in control. Wicked kings and their henchmen would plot evil to their dying day, but still God would rule. The Lord set the limits on the plans of the king. In His own time, God would vindicate His people.

Of Herod and Pilate the Christians prayed, "They did what your power and will had decided beforehand should happen" (Acts 4:27, 28). Centuries before, Daniel had declared the same conviction. The prophet had informed Nebuchadnezzar that his kingdom had been given him by the God of heaven (Daniel 2:37). "He deposes kings and sets them up" (Daniel 2:21, New English Bible).

That God does work in the lives of men is eloquently illustrated in Paul's journey to Rome. For years Paul had prayed that God would open a door so that he might visit the imperial city (Romans 1:8-13). Little did Paul realize that when the Lord granted his request, Rome would pay the fare. The steps of the journey from the appearance of the Roman troops at the temple (Acts 21:27-36), to the escape from the assassination plot (23:12-35), to the shipwreck (27:13-44) all prove that indeed God directs the paths of those who rely on Him (Proverbs 3:5, 6).

Where the Spirit Leads

Anyone who reads Acts and goes away simply impressed with the courage and faith of the early church has missed the main point. Acts is a history of what can happen when the Holy Spirit moves mightily in the lives of men. And that is one thing that time has not changed. The Spirit still lives in the life of His church. He still opens doors, changes lives, motivates His messengers; and today, just as in Acts, the Spirit empowers lives opened to Him in faith.

If there is one thing that Acts can teach us, it is that the Spirit is free. He is never limited by the rules, the power, or even the theology of men. But Acts also shows us that there are some basic concerns that are always high on the Spirit's priority list. There are certain directions toward which He always leads: evangelism, unity, fellowship, self-sacrifice, servanthood, and faith. The Spirit always leads us away from self-satisfaction, indepdendence, division, and short-sightedness.

Acts 29—the Unfinished Task

Acts is really just the prologue. The two thousand years of history that follow are the real story. But whether the twentieth-century church is the conclusion or just one of many more chapters to come, our task reamins the same. The church today must continue the task begun so dramatically by a handful of believers in a little upper room in Jerusalem.

Empowered by the Spirit, we too are to turn the world upside down with the gospel. Acts preserves the pattern begun by Jesus' hand-picked disciples. The resurrected Lord himself provides the means.

May the Lord of glory guide our churches to fulfill our task as ably as did those saints whose lives fill the pages of Acts.

The Spirit has come! The Lord is willing! The task is ours!